Designing Kitchens with SketchUp

ADRIANA GRANADOS

DEDICATION

I dedicate this book to the memory of my mother. I stayed with her through her illness while I was writing. I learned perseverance and dedication from her, and she taught me to never give up, even in the most difficult moments.

Contents

About this book

Welcome to "Designing Kitchens with SketchUp".

Many kitchen designers have used specialized software to make designs fairly quickly. The main benefit of this type of software is its catalogue of kitchen cabinets, as well as the instant pricing information. However, SketchUp is a very powerful tool that can be used for this type of task. SketchUp contains vast library collections that can be found in the 3D Warehouse, the low-cost investment in software needed (even free), and versatility of designs and materials available to apply on surfaces. Any custom design can be approached in a simple way, and designers can grow their own libraries for future use.

In this book you will learn how to drag and drop cabinets that are different sizes, select the door style and finishes, and use plugins to create new components in the blink of an eye. You will also learn other topics such as how to create your own dynamic components with the ability to change size, material and dimensions or create a fast design using pictures or images. If you wonder how you can choose certain items a cabinets company offers, and how to get the detail of the door style and color you want, you will find those answers in this book. Tiles, backsplashes, countertops and a quick exploration adding lighting effects to designs with freeware and shareware alternatives will complete the knowledge you need to succeed in your daily professional life.

Acknowledgements

Thank you once more to Michael Dugas and Jo Dawson for helping me prepare this manual. Michael reviewed content within publication and tested technical content and instruction from his perspective as an Interior Designer. Jo, a longtime newspaper copy editor aware that English is not my mother language, helped me present my ideas and instructions clearly and succinctly.
Also, thank you to Mateo Gaitan for the cover design and constant feedback in many related topics in graphic design.

Downloading Data Files for This Book

Throughout this book exercises were developed that are linked in many cases with others. Due to this circumstance, save each practice with the item number of the chapter. Some elements or models are saved in SketchUp 3D Warehouse. Each chapter tells you whether you need to download them through your Components window. For any question contact sketchup-interior-design@nextcad.net. The author has developed support videos. If you want to access them, send an email to the address above, requesting them; you will receive an invitation to access through YouTube.

Read This before You Begin

This book assumes that the reader has the basic knowledge to work in SketchUp both 2D and 3D. Basic knowledge in the use of the program for interior design was included in my series "SketchUp for Interior Design & Space Planning".

The exercises described in this book have been developed with SketchUp version 8 for Windows, but also include references for use on Mac.

Many of the exercises assume that you are connected to the Internet.

All units are expressed in feet and inches. However, if you are using another unit system you can type the number followed by the unit symbols in the Measurements tool, and all your dimensions will be converted to your template units.

0
Good practice

Configure and save a template for future models: Instead of applying settings every time you start a new drawing, save yourself time and effort by creating a template with the options that do not change between your models. Start a new file. Configure settings as default style, units, Model Info preferences, layers, purge unneeded elements, and set your interface. To save a template file select the Menu > File > Save as Template.

Model close to the origin X,Y, and Z coordinates: Models that have been drawn far from the origin are often difficult to display while using the Orbit tool. If your model looks truncated or disappears, check whether you have elements far away from the origin. In that case use the Zoom Extents tool to check elements far from origin, erase them or move them near it.

Model in Layer 0: The concept of using layers in SketchUp is more related to the visibility of elements than the way they are used in CAD programs. If you decide to work with edges and faces using multiple layers it is very likely that you will end up with hidden elements belonging to different instances. Use layers to control the visibility of groups and components. Once you have modeled all entities in Layer 0 you can create variants of your project by grouping the elements and assigning them to different layers. Assign groups and components only to a specific layer. That way you can control visibility or different project alternatives. Link layer settings to scenes to avoid toggling them on and off.

Draw following inferences: Use red, green and blue axes to stay in the same plane; draw construction lines as guide lines or measurements when needed.

Do not add more detail than needed: The more faces you have the more computer resources you will need. Also, when working with curves reduce the number of segments. This feature can be controlled through the Entity Info dialogue box. Control the display of your elements by hiding the entities that you are not working with. The rendering time will change dramatically.

Importing images to apply as textures: In this book you will learn how to take advantage of images to create cabinets and add details. Using images can slow down your SketchUp model if you use pictures at high resolution. If you need to replace a material for all entities in the selection or in the whole model you might want to take advantage of Global_Material_Change plugin by TIG.

Toggle between different Face Styles to select elements: The X-Ray style will help you to select hidden entities; the Monochrome style will let you see reversed faces; Shaded style will render your model faster.

Reaching the interior spaces: Use Section Plane tool to reach the inside of your model. With just one section plane you can have a front and a back view by reversing it, presented in orthographic or perspective mode.

Group and Components: Keeping your model organized is of special importance when you are designing kitchens. Separating the different parts of your model will save you time and simplify the selection of elements to hide or isolate. Make groups when you are grouping elements that you will work with just one time. Remember to rename each group as soon as you create it; otherwise you will end with countless groups named "Group". You can rename a group through the Outliner or Entity Info window. Use the Outliner to control the organization of your model, nest groups and components, or move your components to a different group. The View > Components Edit > Hide Rest of Model feature is very handy when you want to edit an existing component. In case you want to enter a change to just one component remember to use Make Unique command before editing it.

Create Scenes: To save particular camera views of your model, layers and style settings, shadows, and active section planes.

Shadows: Turn shadows off unless you need to work with them. Shadows take a lot of computer resources.

Use the front face to apply materials: Although when working with textures this variable is not significant, it is when you need to export to other programs like 3D Max or have to work with monochrome style. Check the status of your faces by changing the style to monochrome. To make it more noticeable you can change the color of the faces through the Styles window.

Corrupted files: Recover the last saved version by simply changing the backup file extension from .skb to .skp

1

How to create a kitchen with 3D Warehouse components

In this first chapter you will learn to search for components already developed and stored within the 3D Warehouse, place and move cabinets, interact with dynamic components, and adapt existing items for personal use.

This chapter aims to introduce the general knowledge of using SketchUp to design kitchens. In the market there are several specialized programs that provide the cabinets as part of their libraries. SketchUp provides almost the same options through the 3D Warehouse and everyday more and more manufacturers are adding products to it. The 3D Warehouse is a free, online repository where you can find, share, store, and collaborate on 3D models. It is the easiest way to get your libraries to fill your model. Millions of SketchUp users upload their models and collections for free, so you can find a 3D model of your favorite manufacturer or just about anything you can imagine.

If you need help creating your own catalogs in SketchUp, make them available to designers or have any special request send an email to sketchup-interior-design@nextcad.net.

These exercises also emphasize the use of Outliner. This tool is dismissed by many users of SketchUp. However, consistent use will not only keep your model organized, but it will make your work efficient.

Content

1.1 Create a 3D model from a 2D layout

Design processes usually vary from person to person. However, it is usual to start the first approximation in a 2D floor plan.

In this exercise you are going to begin in 2D. In this case it is better to choose the Top View and Parallel Projection. Use Rectangle and Line tool to draw the walls and the layout indicated in the sketch shown below. Do not draw windows and door openings since these elements are going to be inserted in the 3D model.

Once you have your drawing in 2D you can switch to the Iso view and Perspective mode. Use the Pull/Push tool to bring your walls up to the ceiling height – 9'- 0". Leave the countertop layouts in 2D. These lines will serve you as reference points when placing your cabinets.

To allow an easy way to get inside the 3d model you will practice separating the room and furniture/cabinets in different groups. Managing an interior space sometimes can be tricky especially when you have many objects inside. Separating your model in groups that you can hide or unhide will simplify your design process.

Once you have drawn the walls in the 3D model create guidelines with the Tape Measure Tool. Select windows and doors from the 3D Warehouse and place them in the correct position, aligning with the guidelines.

Finally, you will create a group and rename it as "Layout" inside the Outliner.

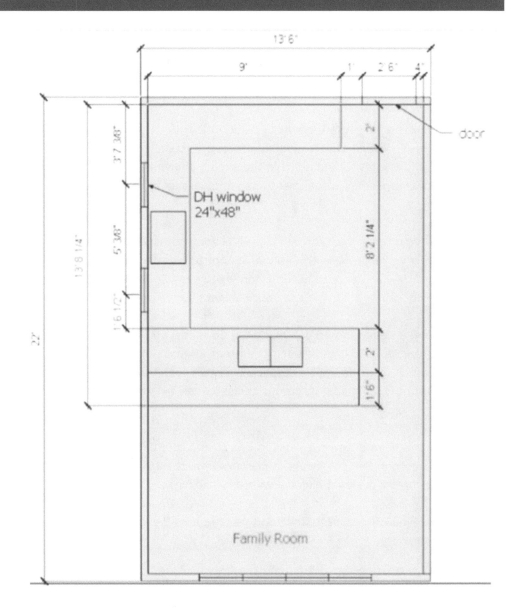

Details

1. **Top** view  .
2. **Camera** > Parallel Projection.
3. **Rectangle** > Click on the screen two diagonal coordinates. Type 13'6",22'. Enter.
4. **Offset** inside > type 4". Enter.
5. Select the **Tape Measure** Tool . Draw guidelines from the inside left edge at 24" and a second one at 7' from the last one, and from the inside top edge at 24", then 8'-2 1/4" from this guide line and another at 24" more.

1-2-3-4

6. Complete drawing according to the given dimensions in the above sketch and the shown pictures below. Do not draw windows yet. Use **Line** tool.

5

6

7. **Create a group** selecting all the entities. Open the **Outliner** and rename it "Layout". Switch to the **Iso** View.
8. **Double-click** inside the group to enter the edit mode. Select the **Pull/Push** tool and create walls of 9' height. **Erase** countertop lines and guidelines.

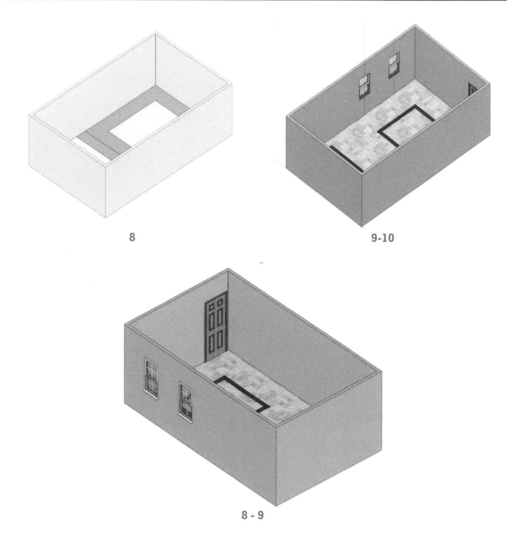

8

9-10

8 - 9

9. **Draw** guidelines to place windows and door according to the floor plan dimensions. Place the sill of windows at 36" from the floor.

10. **Insert** windows by typing dynamic window in the Components window and placing the Scalable Double Hung Window by Google on the wall. At this point you will need to scale it at 24" wide using the Scale tool, gripping center point and typing 24", enter. Create a rectangle on top of the window and use Push/Pull tool to make an opening on both wall faces. Search for the Six Panel Door in the Component window, insert it and repeat the steps to make an opening on both wall faces. **Erase** guidelines. **Close** group. (You can download this starting exercise from the 3D Warehouse by typing "kitchen1.1 by agra".

11. **Save** as Kitchen1.1.

1.2 Drag and drop cabinets of different sizes, select door styles and finishes.

As mentioned before the 3D Warehouse is a website where you can find different 3D models from buildings to robots. It is completely free for everyone to use, and it is getting bigger every day. Anyone can contribute their models to the 3D Warehouse. If you have made something you want to share with others or you would like to advertise your services or products by posting examples of your work, this is where to do it. Companies and individuals have loaded replicas of real world products. You can find objects in the 3D Warehouse by searching directly from the home page or you can locate products doing a standard Google search especially if you include "3D" as part of your Google search. Searching by a product code can save you time by finding objects with specific criteria. Everybody can download models from the 3D Warehouse and integrate them into a specific project. You have many ways to download models from the 3D Warehouse: downloading components using the Components Browser (**Window > Components**.), downloading models using **Get Models** button to access the 3D Warehouse from within SketchUp), downloading models using the 3D Warehouse separate from SketchUp. (visit http://SketchUp.google.com/3dwarehouse) or opening File > 3D Warehouse > Get Models.

Through your search you can get single 3D models or access to collections. In a kitchen project, it is particularly useful to refine your search by selecting "Collections" instead of "Models" from the drop-down menu since you will be able to access a particular manufacturer that may have a certain line through a specific provider, for example Cabinets by KraftMaid® at Lowe's®. You can also obtain access to full kitchen designs and architectural projects. Another option to narrow your search is to include the modifier "is:dynamic" at the end of your search phrase. Dynamic Components in SketchUp are objects - furniture, cabinets, windows - that have been programmed to show specific attributes. You can change dimensions, interact with them, or show different material options. Dynamic Components are shown with a little green arrow inside the thumbnail.

In the next exercises you are going to practice searching for components, learn how to refine your search, download non-dynamic and dynamic components, place them in the correct position, use moldings, interact with and change attributes, and replace components with other ones. In order not to favor one brand over another, the author has developed generic components to be used in the learning process. However, as noted previously, many manufacturers have placed their models in the 3D Warehouse. The components of such brands can be used similarly.

Details

1. **Open** Kitchen1.1. You can also download the file by typing "Kitchen1.1 by agra" through the Get Models option. When downloading components, it is particularly helpful to have a good view of the model to help you position the cabinetry.
2. Once you have your model open select File menu > 3D Warehouse > **Get Models**.
3. **Type** "kitchen by agra" > Search.
4. Change the drop-down menu on top of the page from Models to **Collections**.
5. Click on **Search** button.
6. **Select** Kitchen Cabinets.
7. **Select** Kitchen Cabinets. Note specifications about this particular collection. Green arrow inside the thumbnail denotes that the collection is a Dynamic Component collection.
8. **Choose** Kitchen Base Cabinets. **Select** Kitchen Base Corner Cabinet component and download it into your model. These components are thought to be inserted from the left bottom endpoint. If you need to scale them you will need to grow to the right. While placing it point with the mouse close to the bottom edge of the wall. Do not worry about being accurate; you will move it in a second step to its correct position.
9. With the **Move** tool click on the bottom right corner and move the component inferring with the green axis until you reach the edge of the back wall. Click. Move it again inferring with the red axis to place the component aligned with the left wall.

4-5

Kitchen Cabinets
Kitchen Cabinets to be used...
Updated 27 minutes ago

1 collection

7

18

Kitchen Base Cabinets
[remove from collection]
Kitchen base Cabinets to be...
Updated 28 minutes ago

1 model

8

8

Kitchen Base Corner Cabinet
by Agra
Kitchen base cabinet 36x36....
Download Model

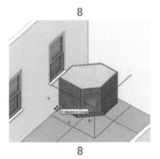

8

8

8

9

10. Now use the **Get Models** icon to access to the 3D Warehouse.
11. **Type** "base double door double drawer cabinet" in the search box. Click on Search button. (You can add "by agra" to refine the search).
12. Make sure that you have the drop-down menu of the 3D Warehouse results showing the "Sort by relevance" option.
13. **Select** Base Double Door Double Drawer Cabinet by Agra. Note the green arrow denoting that this is a Dynamic Component. Download it into your model.
14. With the **Move** tool active click on the upper left endpoint of the cabinet as shown to align it with the right side of the corner cabinet. Zoom in to be accurate. Right-click > Dynamic Components > Component Options > Select 39" for Width < Apply.

■▶ Base Double Door
Double...
by Agra
Kitchen base cabinet with...
Download Model

13   13 -14

15. Open Window menu > **Components**. Type in the search box "base single door by agra". Search >Enter. Select the "Base Single Door and Drawer" component from the list. Note: If you do not see a component on the first page of the list click at the bottom of the dialogue box

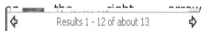

to access to more results. Insert it beside the corner cabinet. You might need to rotate the cabinet. If you hover on top of a component when the **Move** tool is active four red "X" marks will show. Placing the mouse near any of those marks will reveal a protractor indicating that you have a built-in rotation option.

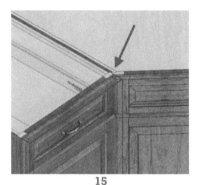

15

Click to reposition the cabinet in the correct angle and move it again inferring with the corner cabinet.

16. While still selected, right click > **Dynamic Components** > **Components Options**. Under Width change to 24" and click on the Apply button. The size of the cabinet will change toward the right. Move it and place it again inferring with the corner cabinet. (Zoom in to get a closer view to be accurate in placing cabinets in the right place. If at any point you realize that cabinets are not positioned correctly, you can

select them and move them again, keeping in mind to align them to the next cabinet).

17. **Type** "pots and pans two drawers cabinet" in the Components window. Click on the thumbnail "by Agra", download the cabinet into your model, rotate it with the Move tool, and place it beside the last one inferring with the front top corner. Check in Dynamic Components > **Components Options** to have the 30"W option.

18. Select the **Move** tool and move the cabinet 31" to leave a space in between for the slide-in oven. While moving select an endpoint, infer with the green axis, and enter 31" in the Measurements box. **Save**.

1.3 Use a 3D Warehouse component and make changes to it to make it suitable for your project.

For the sink base you are going to bring an island saved in the 3D Warehouse and change cabinets types and dimensions. This particular component has different types of doors and the length is too short for this project.

In this lesson you will learn to replace one component with another. To do this you will need to have both components within your model. Then you must select the one you want to change. Next, open the Window Component > right-click on the thumbnail of the new component > Replace Selected. In the next exercise you will swap two different components.

If you have several instances of the same component in your model and you want to select them all open your In Model library. Then right-click on the component that you want to change (inside the Components dialogue box), and choose the Select Instances option.

Details

1. **Type** "KraftMaid kitchen island" in the Components window. Enter. Click on the thumbnail and drop it in your model. Applying the same concepts, rotate and move to locate the island beside the drawers' cabinet as shown in picture 2. Leave 5 1/4" space between the toe kick of the pots and pans cabinet to have enough space to open the drawers and place a filler beside the pots and pans cabinet.

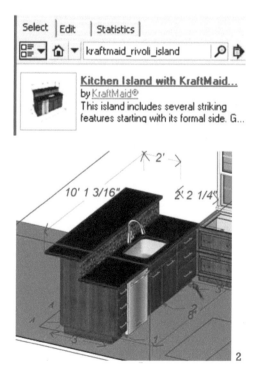

2. **Double-click** on the group with the Select tool active to enter to the edit mode. Erase dimensions. Another alternative to erasing could be to open the Layers dialogue box and turn on hidden layers. (You will still need to erase some dimensions that are on Layer 0). Close Group.

3. **Type** "base blind corner cabinet by agra" and insert it anywhere in your model. (You will erase it in a later step).

4. **Double-click** on the island group with the Select tool active.

5. **Select** the right three-drawer cabinet.

6. Open your Components window and click in **In Model** icon. Locate the Base Blind Corner icon.

7. Right-click > **Replace selected**. The Three-drawer cabinet will be replaced by the corner cabinet.

8. Right click > Dynamic Components > **Components Options**. Select the 45" option. Apply. Close the component.

9. **Move** the island group to realign the Base Blind Corner.

10. **Type** "sink base cabinet by agra" inside the Components window. Download it anywhere inside your model. (You will erase it in a later step).

11. **Double-click** on the island group and select the sink base cabinet.

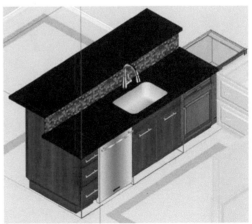

10   11

12. Open your Components window and click in **In Model** 🏠 icon. Locate the Sink Base icon.
13. Right-click > **Replace Selected**. The Sink Base cabinet will be replaced by the new one. Right click > Dynamic Components > Components Options. Select the 36" option.
14. Repeat the same steps searching for "Base 3 Drawers by agra" in the Components window to replace the three drawers.
15. Right click > Dynamic Components > **Components Options**. Select the 12" option.
16. **Erase** all the cabinets that you downloaded to perform the previous steps and sample wood grain to match on the left sides of the Kraftmaid® island.

Note: On your own repeat steps 12 to 14 and replace the existent faucet with another type suitable for kitchens saved in the 3D Warehouse.

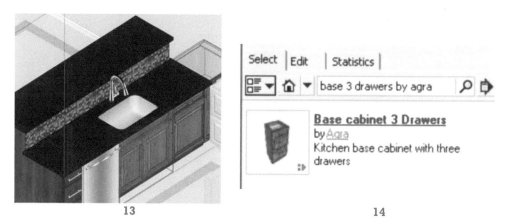

13   14

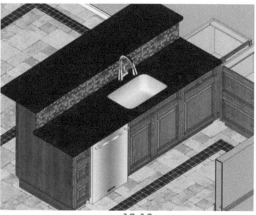

15-16

Note: The next step can be omitted if you are skilled in handling the Orbit tool. However, in order to extend the peninsula countertop in the next steps you will be introduced to the X-Ray mode.

17. Open View menu > **Face Style** > **X-Ray.**
18. **Double-click** the peninsula to enter to the edit mode. **Double-click** again to reach the edit mode of the countertop.
19. With a **crossing window** select the face of the right edge of the countertop.

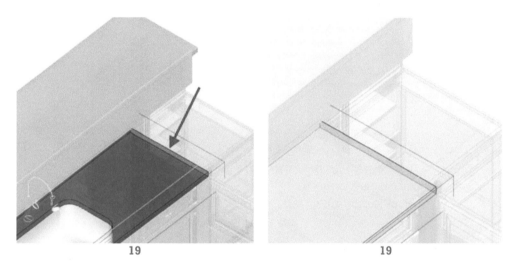

19   19

20. With the **Push/Pull** tool pull out the face until you align it with the back of the pots and pans cabinet.
21. Open the View menu > Face Style > uncheck the X-Ray mode to return to the **Shaded with Textures** mode.

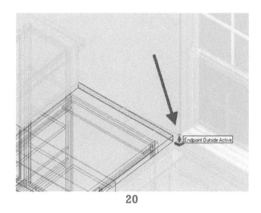

20   21

22. **Type** "wall single door by agra" in the Components window. Download the component.
23. **Double-click** on the island and select the four back panels.
24. Open the **In Model** library, select the component downloaded in step 22, right-click > **Replace Selected**.
25. Right click > Dynamic Components > **Components Options**. Select the 24" option.

22   23

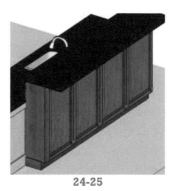

24-25

26. The advantage of working with groups and components becomes noticeable when it is difficult to display items from an appropriate point of view. Since the walls belong to a different group from cabinets, you can hide the walls and keep only the cabinets visible. Click on any wall, right-click > **Hide**.
27. **Double-click** until you reach the island toe kick instance and pull out the face up to the back of the cabinets against the wall.

28. Activate **Move+Ctrl/Opt**. Copy the last cabinet to complete the missing piece under the bar countertop.(You will need to infer the red axis using the Shift key since the cabinets in the Kraftmaid island were created with the "Any" alignment option).
29. Change the width to 21" inside the Component Options window.
30. **Double-click** on the top countertop and pull out the edge to reach the back of the cabinets against the wall level.

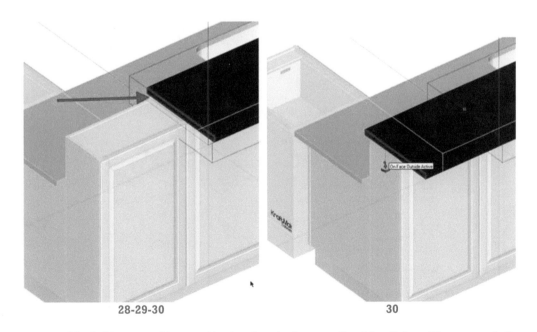

28-29-30   30

31. Orbit around to see the back splash area. Double-click until you reach its instance to enter to the edit mode. **Pull** out ![icon] to extend it to match the countertop edge. Close group.

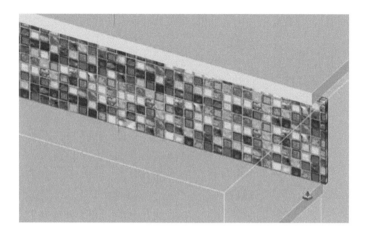

32. **Erase** any component that you have used to replace an existing one.
33. **Type** "slide-in 30" oven by Whirlpool Corporation" and insert model JES9800CAS 30" Slide-in oven aligning with the midpoint of the clearance between the cabinets.
34. **Save as** Kitchen1.3.

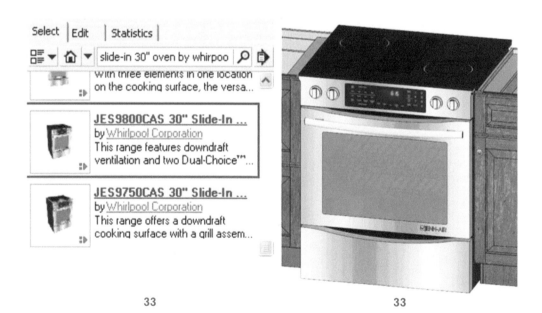

33   33

1.4 Create a new element, sample the material and create a new group.

In this exercise you will create a new countertop, sample the material from the peninsula countertop, and create a separate group.

Details

1. Open the kitchen1.3 file.
2. Activate the **Tape Measure** 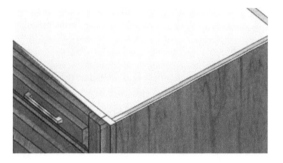 tool and create guide lines inferring with the outside top edge of the cabinets. Once you have created all the required guide lines you can select the cabinets, right-click > Hide to work more comfortable with the Line tool. (You can skip this step if you have good skills with inferences, Zoom-in, Zoom-out and Orbit tool to work just with the Line tool).

3. Activate the **Line** tool. Infer with the 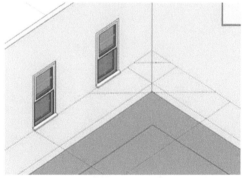 intersection of the guide lines until you get new faces on both side of the oven. For the corner you do not need to follow the angle since the countertop must be parallel to both walls.

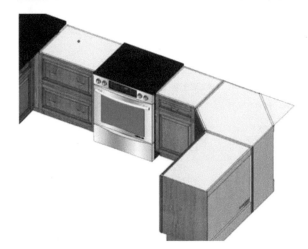

4. **Erase** the guide lines.
5. Click on the corner face. Right-click > **Select** > **All connected**. Right-click > **Make group**.
6. **Double-click** on the countertop group to enter to the edit mode.
7. Select the **Push/Pull** tool and pull up inferring with the same level of the peninsula countertop. Click.
8. Repeat steps 5-7 with the countertop on the left side.

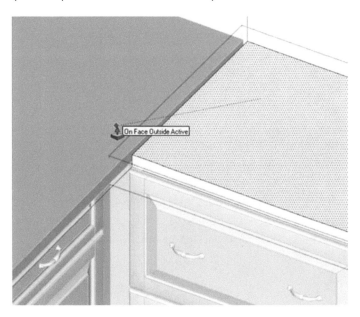

9. Pull out the countertop front edge 1". Close the group. Repeat.
10. Activate the **Paint Bucket** tool. Sample the black countertop material by pressing the Alt/Command key and pointing to the peninsula countertop. **Paint** the countertop. Note that all the faces were painted with just one click. When any group or component was created with the

Default material, a new texture can be applied from outside the group without having to enter to the edit mode.

11. Save as kitchen1.4.

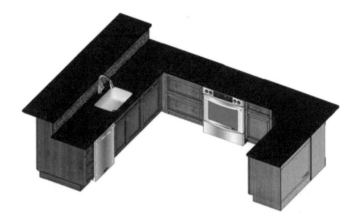

Note: There is a very useful plugin called ThruPaint by Fredo. It belongs to Fredo Tools package and allows you to not only manage textures with different orientations but to paint any component face without entering the edit mode. A must for interior designers.

1.5 How to use section planes to reach the interior of a room and save scenes for ulterior use.

Besides grouping your model in separate parts, the best way to reach the interior of a room is by using section planes. Use the **Section Plane** tool to create section cuts enabling you to view geometry within your model. Activate the Section Plane tool from the Guide Toolbar (Microsoft Windows), the Tool Palette (Mac OS X) or the Tools menu.

You can use the Move tool and Rotate tool to reposition section planes just as you reposition other entities. Using **Reverse cutting direction** allows you to reverse the direction of a section plane. Section planes are active until another entity, such as another section plane, is selected. There are two ways to activate a section plane: double-click on the section plane while in the Select tool or right-click on the section plane and select 'Activate' from the context menu. One section plane can be active for each context in your model. Therefore a section plane within a group or component can be active at the same time because they are in separate contexts to a section plane outside of any group or component. A model that has a group that also contains two other groups has four different contexts (one context outside of any group, one context inside the top level group, and one context each for the groups contained within the top-level group), and can have four active sections at once.

Active Section Plane may be saved to a scene. Section cut effects will animate during animations. You can use Scenes to save camera views, as well as several additional properties. Scenes only store properties, not geometry. There is only one instance of the geometry in a model, and all Scenes are simply views of that geometry. If you have a scene selected and draw some new geometry, you'll see the new geometry on every scene. The only things you can change from scene to scene are the properties that are stored. Components do not have Scenes. If you create a model with Scenes and share it in the 3D Warehouse, and then you download that model directly into a SketchUp model, it comes in as a component. To be able to see and access Scenes, you must open the model in a new instance of SketchUp, so it opens as a full model rather than as a component in a model.

In the next steps you are going to create section cuts and toggle between them to activate one at the time. Then you will create scenes to keep different views.

Details

1. Open Kitchen1.4. You can also get all the resources for this book sending an email to SketchUp-interior-design@nextcad.net . Indicate where you bought the book.
2. Start by checking that **Display Section Planes** and **Section Cuts** in the View menu are not checked.
3. Unhide walls and cabinets using the Outliner window.
4. Create any ceiling design (the example shows a tray above the kitchen area) and create a separate group with those entities.

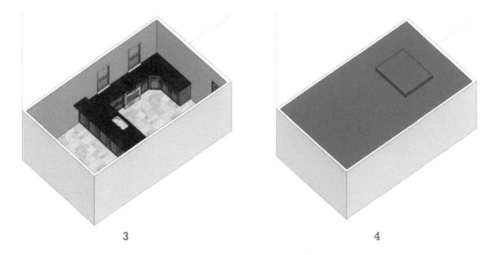

3   4

5. Activate the **Section Plane** tool. Hover with your mouse on the right wall. A green section plane will show.

6. Click. A section cut is created. **Click** on it to select. It should be highlighted in blue color.

7. With the **Move** tool move it toward the inside of the kitchen space.

8. Right-click on the section cut frame > **Align View**. Select Camera > Parallel Projection.

9. Click once on **Display Section Planes** icon   /   to turn off the section plane. To turn on icons select View > Toolbars > Sections.

10. Click once on the **Display Section Cuts** icon   to turn off the section cut. The walls will show hiding the interior of the kitchen. Click on the **Display Section Cuts** icon   to reveal the interior again.

11. Window menu > **Scenes** > click on the Add sign 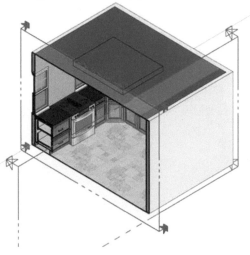 . To the prompt question answer "Save a new style" > **Create scene**. In the field Name write "Left" and click outside. Do not change any properties. Note that a tab named Left was created on the top left corner of your model screen.

12. Click once on the **Display Section Cuts** icon to hide the section along the right wall and select the Iso view.

13. **Repeat** steps 4, 5, and 6 this time placing the section plane on the front wall and moving it between the peninsula and the back cabinets.

14. Select the new section plane. It must turn blue. Right-click > **Align View**. Check that you are still in Parallel projection.

15. Click once on the **Display Section Planes** icon to hide them.

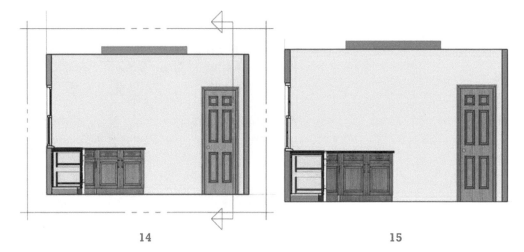

14   15

Note: Use the Toggle Section Cuts toolbar item in the Section Planes toolbar (Microsoft Windows) or Customize toolbar screen (Mac OS X) to hide and unhide section cuts. Additionally, you can use the Toggle Section Plane Display in the Section Planes toolbar (Microsoft Windows) or Customize Toolbar screen (Mac OS X) to hide and unhide Section Plane entities. These controls are helpful in keeping your model uncluttered.

16. Window menu > **Scenes** > click on the Add sign ⊕ . To the prompt question answer "Do nothing to save changes" > Create scene. In the field Name write "Rear" and click outside. Do not change any properties. Note that a tab named Rear was created on the top left corner of your model screen.
17. Return to the Iso view and repeat steps 4,5, and 6 this time placing the section plane on top of the ceiling.
18. Move the section plane downwards and place it below the countertop cabinet.

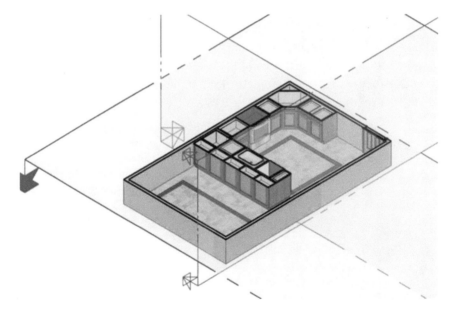

Note: Every time you add a new Section Cut, all of the existing Section Plane objects in your model become visible. The custom style you created doesn't change, though. If after adding a new Section Cut you want to hide all of your Section Plane objects, just choose View > Section Planes from the menu bar.

19. Again, right-click > Align View.

20. Turn off **Display Section Planes** .

21. Window menu > **Scenes** > click on the Add sign ⊕ . To the prompt question answer "Do nothing to save changes" > Create scene. In the field Name write "Floor Plan" and click outside. Do not change any properties. Note that a tab named Floor Plan was created on the top left corner of your model screen.

22. Return to the Iso view. Turn off **Display Section Cuts** to see the complete model.

23. **Select** the ceiling, right-click > Hide.

24. **Select** Layout group, right-click > Hide.

25. Window menu > **Scenes** > click on the Add sign ⊕ . To the prompt question answer "Save as a new style" > Create scene. In the field Name write "Cabinets" and click outside. Do not change any properties. Note that a tab named Cabinets was created on the top left corner of your model screen.

26. **Click** on the "Left" tab to return to that scene. Notice that the section planes are showing again. Turn them off. Right-click on the "Left" tab > Update. To the prompt question answer "Save as a new style". Repeat the same process for tabs "Rear" and "Floor Plan". Now toggle between all the created scenes.

27. **Return** to the "Cabinets" tab. Unhide Layout group using the Outliner. Create a new scene named "Walls".

28. **Save** as Kitchen1.5

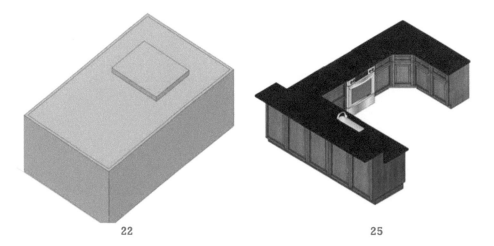

22   25

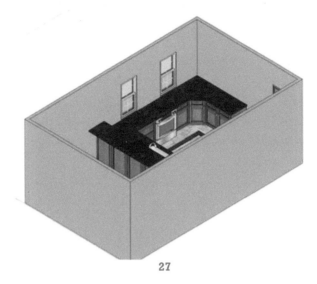

27

Note: In the Scenes window you can find all the visibility properties that you can control when you are adding a new scene. Before creating a scene is a good practice to recheck what the properties that you want to save are.

1.6   How to create a backsplash

The backsplash is a vertical surface that may have different treatments. In the following exercise you will create a surface that will have the same tile as the backsplash of the sink peninsula. You will then create different groups to show different material options controlling visibility by using different layers. You will also practice moving groups using the Outliner, work with nested groups and rename them.

Details

1. **Open** file Kitchen1.5. To access to all the resources files send an email to SketchUp-interior-design@nextcad.net . Indicate where you bought the book.
2. **Click** on the Walls scene tab. **Draw** two guide lines at 18" from the countertop.
3. Activate the **Rectangle** tool and click on the endpoint of the countertop next to the door.
4. Move the mouse to the diagonal corner and click on the intersection of the two guide lines.
5. **Draw** another rectangle on the windows wall inferring with the peninsula top countertop and the opposite corner of the L. The windows will be partially covered by the rectangle, but you will erase those areas in the next step.

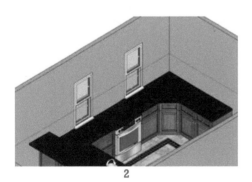

2

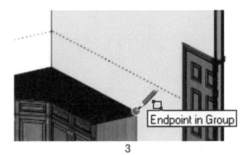

3

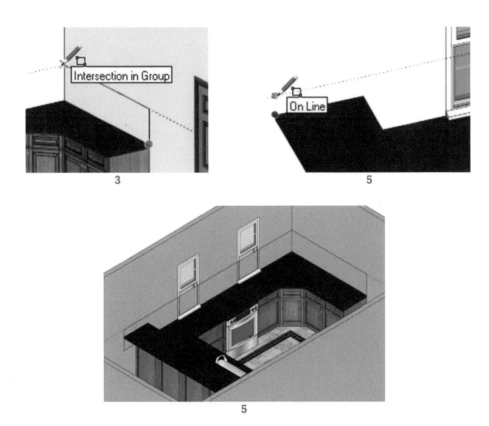

6. Draw **rectangles** on top of each window to separate the backsplash from the area covering each window. **Select** the areas of the rectangles drawn over the windows and **erase** them. Erase the crossing top lines too.

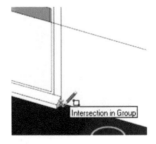

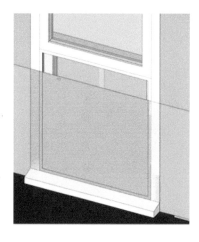 

6

You might also want to cut the area below the peninsula countertop. To do this, activate View > **Face Style > X-ray**. As you learned before this option is very useful when you want to see or infer to hidden lines. Another way is to hide or move the peninsula a distance easy to remember to free the view of this part of the wall, draw the lines, and then move the peninsula back in place. Erase the lines behind the countertop and return to **Shaded with Textures** face style mode.

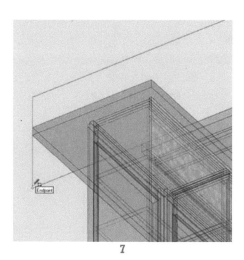 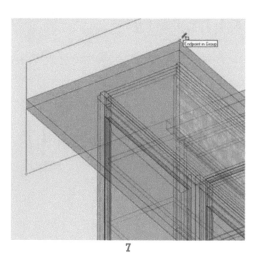

7   7

7. Click on any face with the select tool, right-click > Select > **All connected**. Right-click > **Make Group**. (You could also select all the surfaces by pressing down CTRL/OPT key while selecting with double-click one by one the four surfaces).

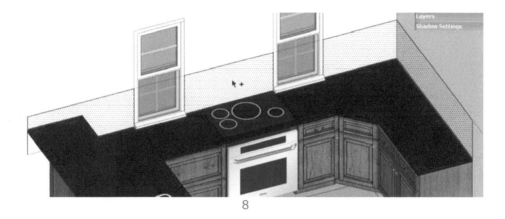

8

8. **Highlight** the backsplash group. Open the **Outliner**, look for the highlighted word, right-click > **Rename**. Type "Backsplash". Click outside the word.
9. **Double-click** on the Backsplash group to enter to the edit mode. Select one face with the **Push/Pull** tool and pull out ½" to provide a thickness to the backsplash. Repeat on every single face. Close group.
10. Select the **Paint Bucket** tool and sample (Paint Bucket + Alt key) the glass tile from the peninsula backsplash. Apply it on the rest of the backsplash.

10 - 11

10 - 11

Note: You can apply any material to a closed group when the faces within the group or component are assigned the default material. It is good practice to leave the default material when you want to show different alternatives with just one click. If you assign any other material while in edit mode of a group or component, you will have to edit it to change for a new one.

11. Click once on the corner countertop to highlight it. Open the **Outliner** window. The word Group will be highlighted too. Right-click > **Rename** > Type "Countertop1". Click outside. Repeat with the second countertop and renaming it "Countertop2".

12. Select the word "backsplash", drag it, and **drop** it inside the Layout group.

13. In your model select the base cabinets, oven, and countertop, right-click > **Make Group**. Right-click again over the word in the Outliner window > **Rename** > Type "Base cabinets".

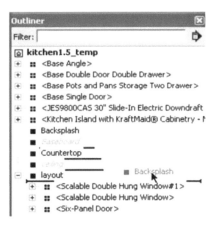
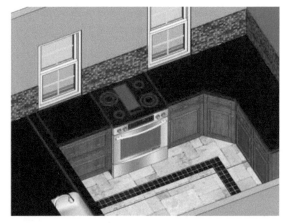

14. Open the **Outliner** and write "back" on the Filter field. The list will show only the Layout word and below the backsplash group in red. Select the backsplash word. (Expand the Layout group to see Backsplash inside).

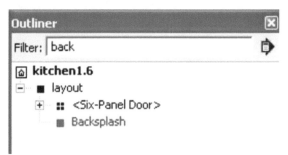

15. Choose the **Copy** tool (Move + Ctrl/Opt) and click once in the corner to select the starting point of the copy. Click again in the same point to drop the copy in the same place. Notice that another "Backsplash" word appears below the first one. Close group.

16. Open the **Layers** window and add ⊕ two new layers. Name them "Alternative 1" and "Alternative 2". In the next step you are going to move both backsplashes to these new layers.
17. Select the first backsplash in the Outliner > right-click > **Entity Info**.
18. Change Layer0 by Alternative 1.
19. Select the second backsplash and repeat steps 17 and 18, choosing this time Alternative 2.

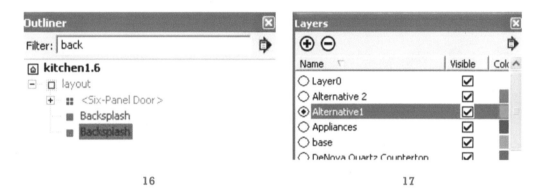

16 17

Now you are going to create a scene for each alternative.

20. Open the **Layers** window and uncheck "Alternative 2" to make it invisible. You should still see a backsplash. If not, open the Outliner to check if the group is hidden.
21. Open **Scenes** window. Create a scene called "Alternative 1".
22. Return to the **Layers** window and turn off Alternative 1 layer and turn on Alternative 2 layer.
23. Open **Scenes** window. Create a scene called "Alternative 2".

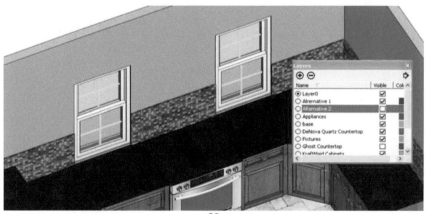

21

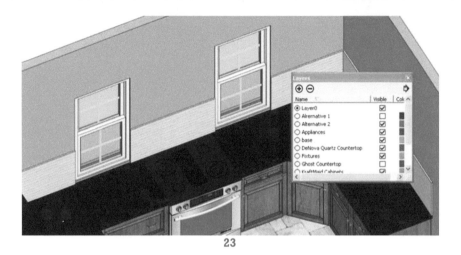

23

24. Type in the **Components** window "Tile sample by Agra" > Search.
25. Download the component to your model. All the materials will be added to your **In Model Materials** window.

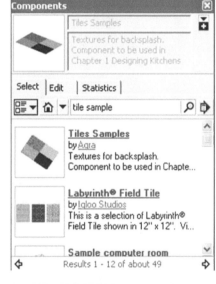

Note: After applying a material Purge Unused to keep the size of your file as small as possible.

26. Select the Alternative 2 **scene**.
27. In the **Outliner** filter refine your search by typing "bac". Look inside the Layout group and select the backsplash word. The backsplash group will be selected within the Layout group.

28. Choose the **Paint Bucket** tool and sample any material from the swatch. Apply the material. (You do not need to enter to the edit mode since the group was created with the Default material.
29. Erase the tile samples swatch component. Purge Unused components and then purge unused materials.
30. Now toggle between "Alternative 1" and "Alternative 2" **scene tabs** to show the two options. **Save** it as Kitchen1.6.

1.7 How to insert wall cabinets

The insertion process for wall cabinets is similar to that for base cabinets. In this exercise you will place the cabinets in conjunction with the top of the walls because it is a guide at the same level for easy location. After you insert all the wall cabinets you can create a group and place it at the new level easily. You may also vary the heights of some cabinets by entering the edit mode of the group and move them up or down. In this exercise you will continue to import 3D Warehouse Dynamic Models. You will also create a single element like a wooden valance over each window. It is recommended that every time you insert a component to place it on the edge of the wall and then zoom in to move it precisely next to the previous cabinet. Note that the cabinets used in this exercise grow to the right, meaning that if you choose a wider one in Component Options the insertion point will remain the same.

Details

1. Open Kitchen1.6 file. You can also get all the resources for this book sending an email to SketchUp-interior-design@nextcad.net . Indicate where you bought the book.

2. **Type** "Wall corner by agra" in the Components window. **Click** on the Wall Blind Corner 39H cabinet thumbnail and place the component on the walls. Do not worry about the space that you have between the countertop and the cabinet bottom; you will move it in a later step. While inserting any cabinet that has been created with "Any" alignment try to place it on a wall face, otherwise the component will not be in the vertical position. After that you can relocate it. Move the cabinet to the wall top corner.

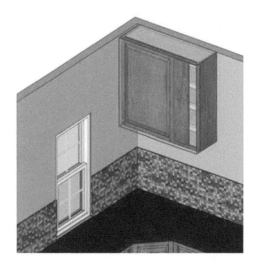

3. With the cabinet selected, right-click > Dynamic Components > **Component Options** > Open Model drop down menu > Select 39", Left > Apply. This component has been created to switch door hand. However, in those cases that you do not have that option, if you want to turn the door hinge hand you can enter to the edit mode, select the door component > right-click > Flip Along > Component's red/green.

4. **Type** "Wall double door by agra" in the Components window. **Select** "Wall Double Door 39H". Place it next to the corner cabinet. Right-click > Dynamic Components > **Component Options** > Open Model drop down menu > Select 36" > Apply. After changing properties you will probably need to relocate it on the wall and use the Move tool to get the correct position. Zoom-in if you need to select the starting point corner.

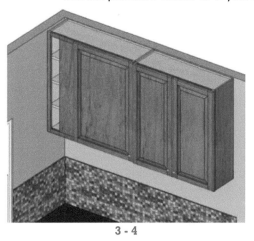
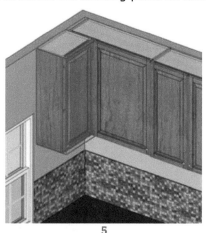

3 - 4   5

5. **Search** for "Wall Single Door by agra" in the Components window and place it on the windows wall next to the corner cabinet. Right-click > Dynamic Components > **Component Options** > Open Model drop down menu > Select 18", Right > Apply. Move it to place it correctly bearing in mind that the cabinet front is bigger than the back.

6. Open again the **Components** window, **type** "Wall Open by agra". Select the Wall Open Cabinet 39H. Insert it. Right-click > Dynamic Components > **Component Options** > Open Model drop down menu > Select 12" > Apply. Align it with the end of the backsplash over the peninsula. You will move this cabinet in a later step. Remember that for aligning an object with another one you can constrain the movement along an axis by pressing down the Shift key and pointing to the endpoint that you want to infer with.

7. **Repeat** the same process inserting from the In Model library a Wall Double Door 39H. Select as Component Options 33".

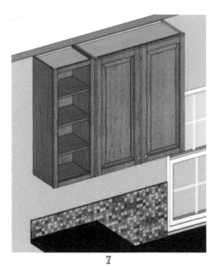

7

8. For the cabinet between the windows type "wall double door 36Hx12" in the **Components** window. **Select** "Wall Double Door Cabinet 12x36H". Place it inferring with the top edge of the wall. You do not need to be exact. You will move it in the next step. Change the Component Options to 33".

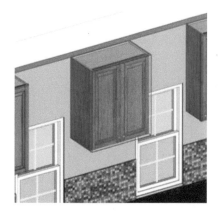

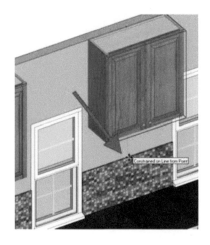

9. Select the **Move** tool and hover your mouse over the cabinet until the tag "Midpoint in Component" appears. Click to select that starting point. Move to infer with the green axis and then hold down the Shift key to lock that direction. Point to the midpoint of the backsplash line below. **Click** to place it.

For the space between the windows you will create a wood valance.

10. **Zoom-in** the area close to the wall corner. Activate the **Line** tool and draw a line across between the two cabinets. Move the Line down > type 12″ > click. Make sure to infer with blue and green axis while you complete a rectangle.

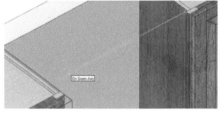

11. Use the **Tape Measure** tool to draw two guide lines at 2″ from the short edges.

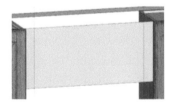

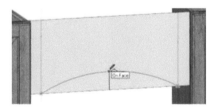

12. With the **Arc** tool draw an arc between the two guidelines with a 3″ bulge.
13. **Erase** the guide lines and the bottom line.

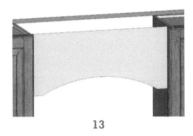

13

14. **Select** with double-click edges and face, right-click > **Make Component** > "valance" > accept the other setting > Create.
15. **Copy** (Move+Ctrl key) the valance to the other side of the cabinet where the second window is.
16. **Double-click** on one valance to enter to the edit mode and with the **Push/Pull** tool provide a ¾" thickness. Close component.

15   16

17. Select the **Paint Bucket** tool + Alt/Ctrl key. Sample the material of a cabinet. Paint the valances.

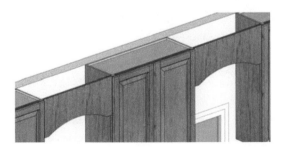

17

18. Move the Double Door cabinet that is close to the peninsula next to the left valance.

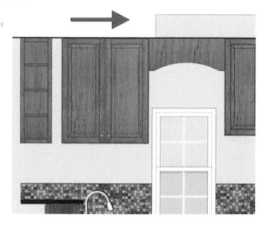

19. Select the Open cabinet > right-click > Dynamic Components > Component Options > Select 15"W.
20. Move the Open cabinet next to the Double Door cabinet.
21. Change to a **Top view** and check to see if all the wall cabinets are in correct position and if the doors have enough space to open.
22. **Select** all the wall cabinets and the two valances, right-click > **Make Group**.

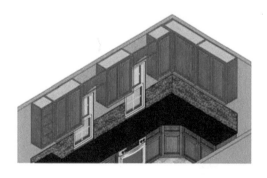

23. With the group highlighted open the Outliner, erase any word in the Filter field, right-click > **Rename** > Wall cabinets.
24. Choose the **Move** tool. Pick as the base point the bottom endpoint of the open cabinet and move the group down inferring with the blue axis to place it matching with the top edge of the backsplash.
25. Save as Kitchen1.7.

1.8　How to create a rosette appliqué using a picture as a texture.

One of the strengths of SketchUp is the ability to create a texture from any picture and distort it to cover any face. While the following exercise is simple in that the image you will use has no perspective distortion, it will provide a methodology to apply pictures of cabinet doors, moldings, or appliqués to any flat surface and add incredible details at no expense to the size of your files or complexity of your models. In this exercise, you will use two images provided by Osborne Wood. The first one will be applied as a texture to a cylinder. Because the tone of the wood is different from the one used in the cabinets you will also learn to sample a color and apply it to the new texture. The second texture is a classic carved wood onlay that has an irregular shape. After creating the texture you will hide the edges of the face that contains the texture. Finally you will create components and save it to your file system for future use. The creation of personal libraries takes time and effort, but once you accumulate components they can be reused in other models. This allows you to create future projects in a very short period of time.

Microsoft Windows

1. Open File > 3D Warehouse > **Get Models** > Type "appliques by agra" > Download Model > Answer "no" to the prompt Load Into Model? > Save it in your computer.
2. Open the downloaded file > Open the **Materials** dialogue window and click on the **In Model** 🏠 button > right-click the Onlay thumbnail > **Export Texture Image** > Select a location > Export.
3. Repeat the procedure for the Rosette texture.

Mac OS X

1. Open File > 3D Warehouse > **Get Models** > Type "appliques by agra" > Download Model > Answer "no" to the prompt Load Into Model. Save it in your computer. Mac does not have the option to export texture images. Since one of the objectives of this exercise is to create a new texture, you will do some steps that can be omitted in your daily work.
2. Click on the Onlay thumbnail and then click on **Edit texture image in external editor** icon. Save the image in your computer from your image editor program. Repeat the same procedure with the Rosette image. You can also right-click > Texture > Edit texture image.

Details

Microsoft Windows

1. **Open** Kitchen1.7
2. **Zoom-in** a valance. Draw **guide lines** at 8" from the top edge and at 2" from both sides.
3. Choose the **Circle** tool and draw a circle of 1.25" radius.
4. Select the **Pull/Push** tool and provide a 5/16" thickness.
5. Open the **Materials** window in the **Edit** tab and click on the Create Material icon ⊕ .
6. **Type** a name like "Rosette".
7. Check the box "**Use texture image**" and browse the image in the location that you exported the texture image or you placed the resources file > Open > OK.
8. Apply the new texture on the cylinder with the **Paint Bucket** tool.
9. Return to the **Edit** tab of the Materials window and change the size to 2 ½" in the first box. The second box will automatically be recalculated. The cylinder should look like the figure below.

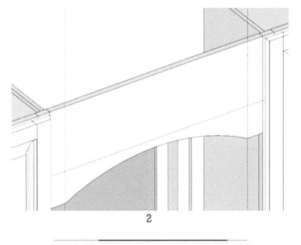

2

3

9

9

10. Click on "**Match color on screen icon**" 🖉 and sample the cabinets color. The thumbnail color will change.

11. Now you will need to adjust the texture position. Select the cylinder top face > Right-click > **Texture** > **Position**. Four colored pins will show. If you instead see four yellow pins right-click again and check "Fix Pins" option.
12. **Drag** to move the texture and place it inside the circle contour. You may need to enlarge the texture a little bit more by using the green pin. Right-click > Done.
13. Sample the cabinet's texture with the **Paint Bucket tool + Alt** and apply it on the edge of the cylinder.
14. Switch to **X-Ray** mode in View menu > Face Style.

11

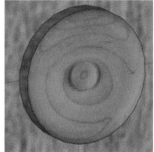
11-12-13

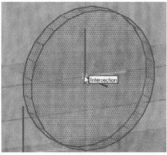
14

15. Select the rosette with a crossing window. Right-click > **Make Component** > Name: "Rosette" > Set Component Axes > locate the axes in the intersection of the two guide lines. Keep the same orientation for the red and green axes > Create.
16. Return the view to the **Shaded with Textures** option.
17. Open the Components window and open the **In Model** 🏠 collection. Scroll down until you see the Rosette thumbnail. **Right-click** > Save As. Browse for the folder where you want to save this component.

Note: You could copy the component in the intersection of the other guide lines, but for the sake of this exercise you will open a local collection.

18. **Click** on the Detail icon 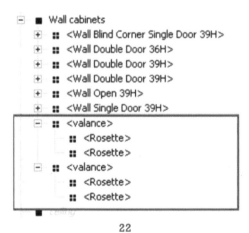 in the Component window. Select "Open or create local collection". Browse for the folder where you just saved the Rosette component > OK. The new collection will open showing all the components saved there.

19. **Select** "Rosette" and insert it in your model on the other side of the valance.

20. To save the path of your new library you can add it to your Favorites.

    Click again the Detail button ⊟ > **Add to favorites**. Your folder will be now listed under "Favorites" when you click ▼ button. (In Mac you have a check box inside the dialogue window).

21. **Erase** guide lines.

22. Finally, select the two rosettes, open the **Outliner,** click on the "+" sign of the Wall Cabinets to open the group, drag them inside the valance component. Pay attention to what valance you choose; otherwise you will end moving the rosettes to the wrong valance and cause wrong placement of the element. Nesting a component inside another component will show the nested component in each instance of the main component.

Mac OS X

1. **Zoom-in** a valance. Draw guide lines at 8" from the top edge and at 2" from both sides.
2. Choose the **Circle** tool and draw a circle of 1.25" radius.
3. Select the **Pull/Push** tool and provide a 5/16" thickness.
4. Open the **Materials** window.
5. To create a new material open the **Color** drop-down menu > **New Texture** > Select the saved image on the beginning of this exercise > Open > Write "rosette" and 2.5" as the width dimension > OK.

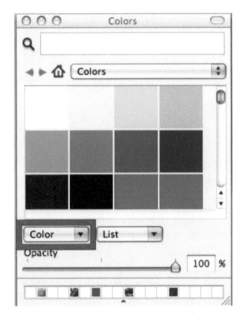

7. Select the **Paint Bucket** tool and paint the cylinder. Since the image is not centered, you may not see any changes to the images yet. (The Match Color on Screen option is not available in Mac. This means that you will need to edit the image using an external editor to adjust the tones of the image).
8. Continue with item 10 to 21 of the Microsoft Windows instructions.

In the next steps you are going to repeat the same procedure but with a classic applique. Since the shape of this applique is not regular you will learn how to insert a texture and hide the edges leaving visible only the picture. This image has been edited before in PainNET but you can use any photoediting program to cut the background. In order to have a transparent background (alpha transparency) the image must have been saved in PNG format.

9. Draw a **rectangle** of 16"x 4" centered on top of the valance. Do not enter in the edit mode yet since you are going to create a separate component and then drag it inside the Wall Cabinets group.

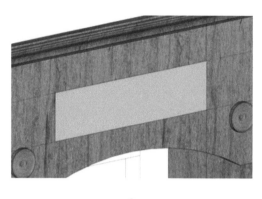

9

10. Open the **Materials** window in the Edit tab and click on the Create Material icon ⊕.
11. **Type** a name like "Classic Appliqué".
12. Check the box "**Use texture image**" and browse Onlay.png in your resources file. Open. OK. Correct the size to 16" x 4".

13. Click on **Match color on screen** icon 🖳 and sample the cabinets' color. The thumbnail color will change.

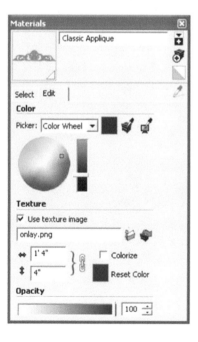

14. Select the **Paint Bucket** tool and paint the rectangle.
15. Now you will need to adjust the texture position. Select the rectangle face > Right-click > **Texture** > **Position**. Four colored pins will show. If you instead see four yellow pins right-click again and check "Fix Pins" option.
16. Drag to move the texture and place it inside the rectangle. Right-click > **Done**.
17. Select the rectangle > Right-click > **Make Component** > Write "Onlay" for Name > Create.
18. **Double-click** to enter to the edit mode. Select **Erase** tool and press-down the **Shift** key to hide the four edges of the rectangle. Close the component. If you do not see the image clearly move it forward 1/16".
19. Select the component again and open the **Outliner**. You will see the word "Onlay" highlighted. **Drag** it inside the corresponding valance component.
20. Save it as Kitchen1.8

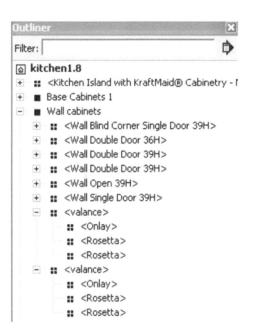

Note: If you are planning to create a presentation with shadow settings, turn off "Cast shadows" of this type of component using the Entity Info dialogue box. Otherwise, the alpha transparency background could cast shadows on other surfaces.

1.9 How to create a crown molding for the kitchen cabinets.

Many times during the design process you will find that you want to add some details, change a cabinet, alter it or add some height to enhance your design. In this exercise, you will use a crown molding profile stored in the resources folder to create a molding on top of the cabinets. You will also raise the cabinet between the windows from the current level. It is convenient to keep in your library profiles of the most used in your designs. Within the 3D Warehouse you may find profiles that have been drawn in millimeters. If you download one of these profiles do it in a separate file. Make adjustments using Scale and explode all the instances of components that can be nested. Position the axes at the base point that you want to use as insertion origin and save the file. This way you can bring it to any model as a component with the measure units that you always work with.

Also note that when you replace one component with another, both elements must be within the In Model library. That is why the new component should be placed inside your model but it does not need to be in the correct location. Once you have inserted a new component in your model it will be added automatically to the In Model library.

Details

1. Open file Kitchen1.8. You can also get all the resources for this book sending an email to SketchUp-interior-design@nextcad.net . Indicate where you bought the book.
2. Start by replacing the 12" cabinet by one of 15" deep. Open the **Components** window and type "wall double door 15x36h". Select the Wall Double Door cabinet and download into your model.
3. Place it anywhere to add it to the **In Model** library.
4. **Double-click** on the Wall Cabinets group and select the cabinet between the two windows.
5. Open the **In Model** collection and search for Wall Double Door 36Hx15 component.
6. **Right-click** > Replace Selected.

4

6   7

7. Select the **Move** tool and raise the cabinet 6" up. Close the group.

8. **Download** from the 3D Warehouse "crownmolding74632.96". This profile was originally in DXF format. It has been modified as explained in the above introduction for your use in this exercise. Place the profile on one corner of the 15" cabinet and rotate it to the correct position.

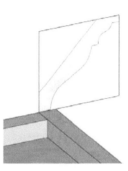

Note: Some manufacturers have developed many of their products for SketchUp, and they are available in the 3D Warehouse. You can also find furniture legs, cornices, brackets and corbels in their websites. If you plan to use any of these 3D models download the DXF version to import it into SketchUp. You will experience fewer issues with faces and edges.

9. Double-click the profile component to enter to the edit mode and draw with the **Line** tool the path for the Follow Me tool on the three exterior edges of the cabinet.

10. Select the three lines and choose the **Follow Me** tool. Click once on the profile face to create the crown molding.

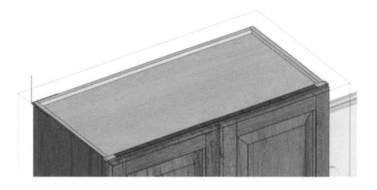

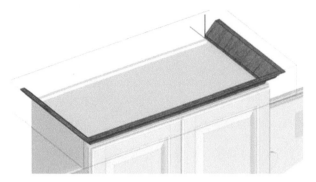

11. **Close** the component.
12. Download the crownmolding74632.96 component again and place it at the end of the left valance.
13. **Repeat** steps 9 and 10 to obtain the result shown below.

12   13

14. Repeat again the same steps, now placing the crown molding profile in the close-to-the-door cabinet corner.

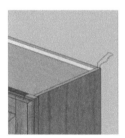

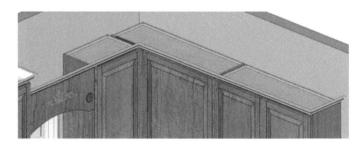

15. **Sample** the wood grain from the cabinets using the Paint Bucket tool + Alt/Command and then apply the texture to the crown moldings.

21. **Erase** any replacement cabinet that you might still have outside the wall group.
22. **Save** as Kitchen1.9

1.10 Fillers and toe kicks.

At times you will need to use filler strips to cover gaps between cabinets and walls. Many are already saved in the 3D Warehouse and some of them are Dynamic Components that can be modified according with your needs. Fillers are essentially pieces of wood. For the sake of this exercise you will hide all the necessary components using the Outliner to reach the toe kick area between the drawers' cabinet and the peninsula and create your own geometry.

Details

1. **Open** Kitchen1.9.You can also get all the resources for this book sending an email to SketchUp-interior-design@nextcad.net . Indicate where you bought the book.
2. Select the Cabinets **scene** tab.
3. **Orbit** around to allow a bottom view of the cabinets between the peninsula and the drawers.
4. **Draw** with the Line tool a rectangle to allow the same height of the rest of the toe kick.

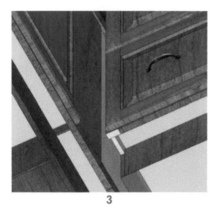

3

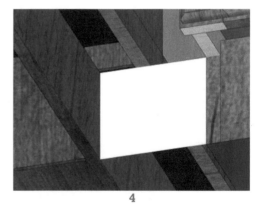

4

5. Draw another rectangle between the cabinet door and the peninsula to allow a filler between the two cabinets.

6. Then with the **Pull/Push** tool provide the same height as the cabinets reaching the bottom of the countertop.
7. Select all the entities > right-click > **Make Group**.
8. **Sample** the wood grain with Paint Bucket tool + Alt/Command and apply the texture on the group.
9. Select the filler, open the Outliner > right-click > **Rename** > name it "Filler".
10. **Drag** the Filler word inside the Base Cabinets group.

7-8

9-10

11. **Save** as Kitchen1.10

1.11 Interact Tool

From the beginning of this chapter you have been inserting Dynamic Components. Any SketchUp Component can be turned into a Dynamic Component and you will learn how in another exercise. To create and edit Dynamic Components, you need SketchUp Pro 7 or higher. Some Dynamic Components are created by manufacturers and resellers to promote their products. Dynamic Components "work" in different ways based what the person who created them wants them to do. But basically you can interact with Dynamic Components in different ways. One is by using the Interact tool.

You can click on a component to make it do what it is set up to do (animate, go to a scene, change colors, etc). If a Dynamic Component is set up to react to the Interact tool, the Interact tool cursor will change its appearance when you move over the component. It will look like this:

Details

1. Open Kitchen1.10 file. You can also get all the resources for this book sending an email to SketchUp-interior-design@nextcad.net . Indicate where you bought the book.
2. Select **Tools** on the top menu > **Interact**.
3. Click on any door that shows the icon shown above. The door will open showing the inside of the cabinet.

1.12 Tips to finish you model.

Flooring

Applying the learned concepts, hide all the groups except for the Layout. Double-click to enter the edit mode. Erase the lines on the floor that you draw on the beginning. Find an image of your favorite tile provider, a brochure that you can scan or a picture that you already have. Create a new texture. Have in mind that when applying a texture like tile, look for an image that already has the grout lines. That image will be repeated to cover all the floor surface. If you choose only one tile the resulting texture will not show the grouts. You can even try to create different areas or designs on the floor and apply different materials. Purge unused materials after you have inserted your selection.

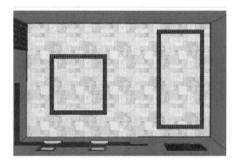

Baseboard

Proceed as you did with the crownmolding except that you will need to find the appropiate profile. If you need further assitance there is a complete exercise in "SketchUp for Interior Design and Space Planning book, Course 2". Make a separate group, rename it and drag it inside the layout group using the Outliner.

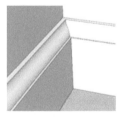

Furniture

Insert components such as a table, lighting, refrigerator and other fixtures. Open the Layers window inside the Window menu. Create a new layer and rename it "Furnishing" if you do not have any for that purpose. Right-click while all the components are highlighted and select the Entity Info option. Change the elements to the new layer. It is very important that when you are structuring your model to think how you are going to use scenes. Since in the next exercises you will have an architectural elevation with no furnishing, placing them in one layer will allow you to hide them when you are using a specific scene. Turning on or off the appropriate layers before creating or updating a scene will work even if you have nested groups.

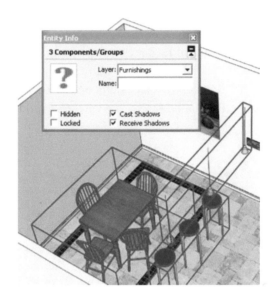

Looking through windows

SketchUp has been used to build models essentially viewed from the outside and the relation of the model typically flows from outside to inside. In interior design the exterior view is one of the elements that enrich our experience of space. Showing outer space through windows and openings in a convincing way can sometimes be a challenge. Here are two approaches for managing a background that can be seen through windows and can work fine when creating scenes, renderings and animations.

The first way is to create a Style that has a watermark used as background with "Stretch to Fit the Screen" settings. The background image can always be seen through translucent surfaces. The downside of this option is that the background should have the same eye level as the perspective you are using. Another drawback may be that many times you want to hide the ceiling and turn on the sunshine to add more contrast to your scene. In that case the background will be seen from inside like the sky shown in the picture below. However, you could still use this option if you create a ceiling with "no cast shadows" properties or a transparent material applied to the outside face. In this way the ceiling would cover the unwanted part of the image but would let the sunshine come in.

The second way is to create a curved surface (it will give a sense of depth) painted with a projected texture of an exterior picture. This element after grouping can be placed at the height you want to solve the problem of eye level height.

In the picture below sunshine was activated with setting in June at midday (to make the sunshine light as vertical as possible). UTC was also changed for this purpose. The model still has no ceiling but it shows a white uniform surface, and shadows add a completely different look and feel of the room.

In the event you have a design or color on the ceiling you want to show you can create a group with "no cast shadows" properties set through the Entity Info Dialogue Box.

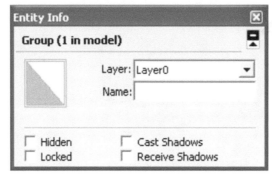

Note: You can get all the resources for this book sending an email to SketchUp-interior-design@nextcad.net . Indicate where you bought the book.

2

How to create a kitchen from pictures and images

In this exercise you will learn how to use pictures and images to create a quick approach to your design and discuss your ideas. Most suppliers of kitchen cabinets have pictures of the type of front doors, colors and designs they offer. If you intend to create a design using a specific brand of cabinet, it can be helpful to use the manufacturer's website to access its online catalogue. You can also scan the pictures from a printed catalogue. Normally the online catalogues have the front images ready for use in SketchUp in the form developed in this exercise.

There are several aspects to be taken into account when creating libraries of images to be applied on a face in SketchUp. The first advice is to get front images without distortion of perspective. These images are easier to manipulate and position on a face. This does not mean that if you have a photo of a kitchen with cabinets you want that you cannot use them. It simply means that sometimes you will have to spend more time adjusting them. Another useful tip is to name the materials so you can easily identify them by manufacturer, color and model. It will save you time when specifying your material list.

This exercise omits the creation of a 3D model. You will download it from the 3D Warehouse in a state of initial drawing. Notice when you open the model that it has only boxes representing the cabinets. The most complex geometry that has been drawn is a crown molding that can be erased if you wish. Adjacent rooms were simulated with other images. This strategy is useful for remodeling projects in which a photo of the site can add a dramatic touch of realism. The ceiling was not included as part of the scope of this exercise. The images used in this exercise are from Merillat Masterpiece® cabinets collection. The images were scanned, edited and cropped with Paint.Net.

Content

2.1   How to prepare your images and create a material.
2.2   Download the model from 3D Warehouse.
2.3   Explore how the model is organized.
2.4   Creating scenes for elevation views.
2.5   How to apply textures to simulate door cabinets and appliances.
2.6   How to create a wood grain from an existing image.

2.1 How to prepare your images and create a material.

The first image explains the type of image best suited to work with the method developed in this exercise. Note that it is a completely front view without any perspective distortion. The next two images have been cut from the first image to simulate doors and drawers. These images have already been included in the In Model material collection of the file that you will work with.

The following steps are the ones that you should follow anytime you want to use a real world texture that you picked for a design. You will need to take a picture of a scaled sample, use any software for editing images, save it in any folder on your computer and finally create a new material as it is described in this exercise.

Details
Microsoft Window

1. Download from the 3D Warehouse "Kitchen2 resources by agra" and open the file (do not download it as a component).
2. Open the downloaded file > Open the **Materials** dialogue window and click on the **In Model** 🏠 button > right-click on a thumbnail > **Export Texture Image** > Select a location > Export. Repeat with all three.
3. Open the **Materials** window in the Edit tab.
4. Click the icon **Create Material** 📦 .
5. Check the box **Use texture image**.
6. **Browse** for the saved image named alina_cherry-natural. **Open**.

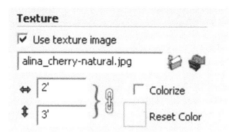

7. Type "Cherry_Natural_Do&Dr" in the material name field and change the dimensions to the real world size.

8. Click on the **OK** button. The new texture will be incorporated into the In Model window. Note that thumbnails belonging to the textures used in the model have a triangle in the lower right side of the icon while the thumbnail that you just created has no triangle. This means that this texture has not been used in the model.

9. **Right-click** on the created texture thumbnail. **Save as**. **Browse** for your library folder. **Write** "Cherry_Natural_Do_Dr.skm" in the File name. Click on the **Save** button. In doing this you have started your own library where you can add all the materials that you usually work with for kitchen design.

10. If when you apply it does not have the appropriate scale you will need to go back to the **Materials** window. Open the **Edit** tab. Click on the **Chain** button to unlock it. Change the dimensions. The texture will show the changes. This dimension relates to the real dimension of the picture that you have from the real world. If you have a tile that is 12"x12" but a picture that has 2 tiles by 2 tiles, you should write for dimensions 24" on each field.

11. Repeat the same procedure to create a door material named Cherry_Natural_Door and a drawer material called Cherry_ Natural_Drawer using Alina_cherry-natural_door.jpg and Alina_cherry-natural_drawer.jpg that you should have saved in item 2 of this exercise.

Mac OS X

1. Download from the 3D Warehouse "kitchen2 resources by agra" and open the file (do not download it as a component).

2. Click on one thumbnail and then click on **Edit texture image in external editor** icon. Save the image in your computer from your image editor program. Repeat the same procedure with the three images. You can also right-click > Texture > Edit texture image.

3. Open Window > **Materials**.

4. Open the **Color drop-down** menu. Select **New Texture**.

5. **Browse** for the alina_cherry-natural image. **Open**.

6. Type "Cherry_Natural_Do&Dr" in the material name field. Provide real world dimensions.

7. Click on the **OK** button. The new texture will be incorporated to the **In Model** window.

8. **Select** the **List drop-down** menu and choose the **Duplicate** option. **Save as**. **Browse** for your library folder. Assign the name of your collection. The Colors window is now open to the new collection.

9. In case you want to create a new material starting from any other material, right-click on any thumbnail and select **Duplicate**.

10. Name the new material, in this case "Cherry_Natural_Do_Dr"

11. Right-click on the thumbnail and select **Edit** option. Make changes and close.

12. If you apply the texture and it does not have the appropriate scale you will need to go back to the **Materials** window, edit it and click on the **Chain** button to unlock it. Change the dimensions. The texture will show the new changes. This dimension relates to the real dimension of the picture that you have from the real world. If you have a tile that is 12"x12" but a picture that has 2 tiles by 2 tiles, you should write for dimensions 24" on each field.

13. Repeat the same procedure to create a door material named Cherry_Natural_Door and a drawer material called Cherry_Natural_Drawer using Alina_cherry-natural_door.jpg and Alina_cherry-natural_drawer.jpg that you should have saved in item 2 of this exercise.

Tip: If you want to reuse an image that is used in a SketchUp material, you can change the .skm extension to .zip. You can then open the bitmap file directly in your file manager or with a decompression program.

2.2 Download the model from 3D Warehouse

The 3D Warehouse is not just a repository of objects to insert into your project. It contains thousands of buildings and projects developed by other users. On many occasions you may benefit from using them as starting point for a new project or as a vignette where you can show your ideas. As mentioned above a 3D model has been created for you to apply the knowledge you will acquire in this chapter. To download the complete model:

Details

1. **Open** a new file.
2. In the Window menu select the option **Components**.
3. Type in the **search** box "Kitchen2 by agra".
4. **Save** the file in your computer. Do not download as a component; otherwise you will need to explode it before starting to use it and additionally losing the scenes that have been prepared for you.
5. **Open** Kitchen2 file that you saved in your computer.
6. **Open** the Materials In Model library and purge unused material if the option is not grayed. You will notice that even though you do not see some materials applied in the model there are some that show that are used in the model. This is the case of Quartz collection that was placed in your model so you can apply in a later step all those materials. A good trick that works when you use frequently the same materials is to create a swatch that includes an image of each of these materials. That swatch can then be imported to any model as a component. Thus these materials will be incorporated into the In Model collection and all you have to do is adjust the measures in the Edit tab of the Materials window if required.
7. Select **View** menu > Face Style > **X-Ray**. Zoom-in the tall cabinet close to the sink. You will see two swatch samples hidden inside the geometry. One is for Quartz that you will use for the countertop material and the other contains a white door from Merillat, a dishwasher, a refrigerator, and a microwave.
8. Turn off the X-Ray mode.

2.3　Explore how a model is organized.

Besides exploring the types of materials that are embedded in a model, you might want to save them for future use. There are several ways that you can explore how a model is organized. The most intuitive way is clicking the mouse on different entities. The model we are using contains several groups according to the process to be done later. To become familiar with the groups use the Outliner. Exploring using the Outliner will give you a better idea how the author organized the model and you will be able to fix errors and reorganize the file the way you want.

Details

1. Menu **Window> Outliner**.
2. **Click** on each word to see the highlighted group.
3. **Click** on the "**+**" sign next to Molding. The hierarchical tree will unfold revealing the content of the two groups of the crown molding cabinets. Repeat the steps for each group. Do not unhide any group yet.

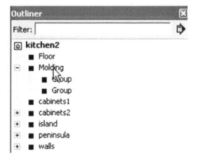

2.4   Creating scenes for elevation views.

To apply textures on faces and then reposition them you should use a suitable point of view to manipulate and adequately position the pins. Having scenes for each elevation can save you time and gives you the opportunity to print them as part of your documentation. The Kitchen2 model already has three scenes that you may select by clicking on the different tabs above the drawing area. "Window" contains the left elevation, "Fridge" shows the right elevation, and "Open Space" shows the front elevation. In this exercise you will create a scene from the rear elevation where the stove is.

Details

1. Select the **Iso** view .

2. Click on the **Display Section Planes** icon to reveal the different section cuts belonging to the three elevations. Turn them off by clicking again on the icon.

3. Click on the "Window" tab. If you do not see the inside of the kitchen

    activate the **Display Section Cuts** icon . Turn off **Display Section Planes** if the section plane is showing.

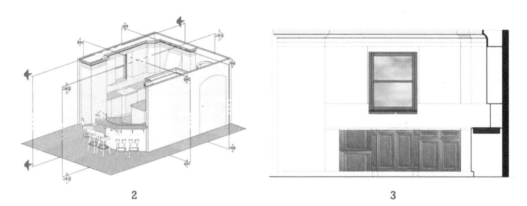

2   3

4. **Select** the "Fridge"tab and then the "Open Space" tab to toggle to the other elevations. Return to the "Window" tab.

5. Now you will create a new scene for the back elevation where the cook top is. Turn off **Display Section Cuts** , choose the **Iso** view and activate the **Section Plane** tool .

6. Place it on the tall cabinet side as shown to **align it** facing toward the back wall. Click. Pay attention to the side the section plane is pointing at. If it is not looking toward the back cabinets right-click > Reverse.

7. **Select** the new section cut and move it toward the back, placing it between the island and the countertop.

6

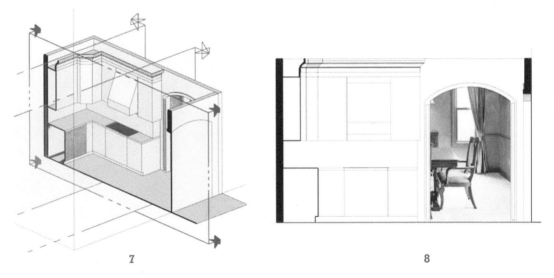

7   8

8. Right-click > **Align View**. Turn off **Display Section Planes**.
9. Open the Scenes window. Click on the **Add Scene** button > Do nothing to save changes > **Create Scene**.
10. **Rename** it for example as "cooktop" and provide a description.

2.5 How to apply textures to simulate door cabinets and appliances.

Applying textures and materials in SketchUp is simple and intuitive. The only difficulty you may experience is that the scale of the chosen material does not match the actual dimensions of the object you are intending to modify. To do this you will need to change its size from the editing tab of the Materials dialogue box. Another variable that you might need to modify is the position of the texture within the area applied. For this you should generally use the function Fixed Pins.

Details

1. Click on the window tab to return to the left view.

2. Click on the Details ⬛ button in **Materials** window > Open or create a collection > Browse for the folder where you saved the door textures created in item 2.1.

3. With the **Select** tool ▶ active double-click on the base cabinet group to enter to the edit mode.

4. Activate the **Paint Bucket** tool ✍. Search for Cherry_ Natural_Do_Dr. Paint the base cabinet at the right of the window.

5. **Select tool > Right-click** on the face > **Texture** > **Position**. Four colors pins will show. If you see yellow pins instead right-click again and check Fixed Pins. The face where the material was applied will show crispy while the contours will show dull.

6. **Drag** the texture to match the red pin to the lower left corner of the rectangle.

7. **Click** the green pin to release it and place it at the end of the second dull image on the right.

8. **Drag** the green pin to the left to match the bottom right corner of the cabinet rectangle. The pin will snap in the intersection of the two lines.

9. **Drag** the blue pin up to match the upper left corner. Adjust any tweak with a correspondent pin.

10. **Right-click** > Done.

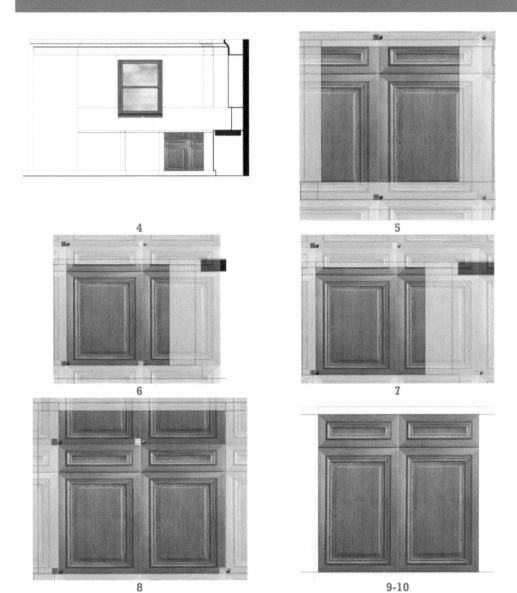

4

5

6

7

8

9-10

11. Repeat the same steps for the cabinet under the sink applying as texture Cherry_Natural_Door. Place two doors inside the rectangle.

12. For positioning the texture on the sink chamfers you do not need to lift the green pin up to the second tiled image. You will only need to drag it to the bottom right corner, and then repeat the step for the blue pin.

13. Apply the same concept on both chanfers.

14. Orbit around to see the result.

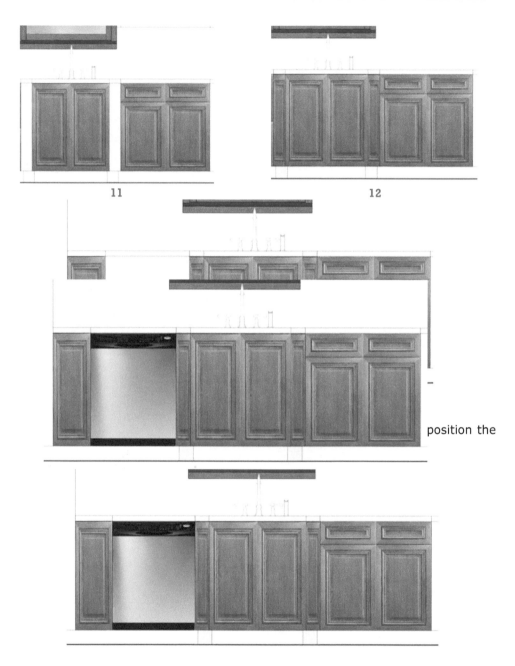

11

12

position the

15

16. Click on the Fridge **scene** tab. Turn on **Display Section Cuts**.
17. **Double-click** the cabinet group to enter to the edit mode.
18. Select from the **In Model** collection the Samsung refrigerator material and reapply it on the big rectangle as shown in the Right Elevation image below, following the same steps.

19. Repeat the same steps with the Bosh microwave and oven to replace these appliances on the right of the refrigerator.

Note: Having acquired the previous knowledge paint the rest of the faces as shown in the images below. Be sure to double-click on each group to enter to the edit mode. If by chance you paint a face while a group is closed you will end applying the same material to the entire group. Just undo the last step and proceed as explained. If you are applying a texture on a similar face that has the same dimensions you can use the Paint Bucket tool + Alt key to sample the material and then paint the new face. Use the quartz materials to apply any that you like on the countertop and practice the same steps with MountainMist white materials to get a different alternative.

Left elevation

Rear Elevation

Right Elevation

Peninsula Elevation

2.6 How to create a wood grain from an existing image.

The variety of grain and color of the wood can be infinite. Using door images applied to faces is very suitable for large panels and doors. However, the fillers and small areas should be painted with the same grain, and may not be available as an image of wood for your project. A simple way to create a material using the same wood of the panels is to edit an image used in a cabinet with any photo editor. This procedure involves a photo editing application such as Paint.net (a free application) or any other photo editing program similar to Photoshop. In the version for Windows, users have an option called Match Color on Screen. Mac users will probably need to use another editing program to get the right tone resembling the cabinet doors. You can link your external image editor to SketchUp so that when you need to edit an image you can quickly access it. To do this on PC just configure Window> Preferences> Applications and write the path. In Mac, set SketchUp> Preferences> your Application on Mac. In this exercise use any editor or Paint.Net to crop a representative portion of the wood grain, save it on your hard drive and then use the new image in the creation of a new material.

Details

Microsoft Windows

1. Window> Preferences> **Applications**. Set the path for your external image editor.
2. Open the **In Model** 🏠 materials library.
3. Search for the Cherry_Natural_Door, right-click > **Edit Texture Image**. The external editor should open.
4. Select the internal raised panel > Image > Crop to Selection.
5. File > **Save as** > type "Wood Cherry Natural" and browse for your library location to save the image.

4

4

6. Open the **Materials** window.
7. Click the icon **Create Material** .
8. Check the box **Use texture image**.
9. **Browse** for the saved image Wood Cherry-Natural. **Open**.

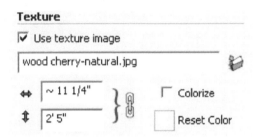

10. **Type** a name in the material name field as Cherry Natural.
11. **Unlock** the aspect ratio keychain and modify the width to 12" and height to 3'-6" (if you cannot unlock, apply the material and then return to the Edit tab to retry changing dimensions).
12. Click on the **OK** button. The new texture will be incorporated to the **In Model** window.
13. If you want to save it for future use, right-click on the thumbnail. **Save as**. Browse for your resource folder. Write "Wood Cherry Natural.skm" in the File name. Click on the Save button.
14. Apply the material on the rest of areas not yet painted, such as moldings and toe kicks.

Note: For the crown molding you can avoid editing the group and apply the texture to the closed group. Note here that the grain of the wood was set vertically and shall be applied so to the crown molding. If you want to be thorough instead of applying the texture to the closed group you should enter the edit mode, apply the material on one face, use the green pin to rotate the texture 90 degrees and then use the blue pin to conceal the edges of clearings dark image. You can sample the modified texture with Paint Bucket tool + Alt and then apply the material to the rest of the faces with Paint Bucket tool + Shift key. You could also rotate the image that serves as a reference for the texture in your editor and save it there as a new image. In that case in SketchUp change the texture image to your new one.

By using the plugin **Make Unique Texture ++** by Aerilius you can avoid most all the previous steps. The plugin offers two options. **Crop texture to selection** creates one new texture. **Make selected face(s) unique** creates for each *elected face its own unique texture with best-fitting bounding box and bakes the UV distortion into it.*

By using the plugin ThruPaint by Fredo you can avoid all these steps and apply the material to the closed group. ThruPaint resides within a suite of tools that Fredo calls FredoTools. This toolset is available for free on the SketchUcation forums. With this plugin you can choose different texture transformations such as rotation, mirror, or tiling.

Mac OS X

1. SketchUp > Preferences> **Applications**. Set the path for your external image editor.
2. Open Window > **Materials**.
3. Search for the Cherry_Natural_Door in the Colors In Model window. Double-click on the thumbnail > **Edit Texture Image in external editor** button. The external editor should open.
4. Select the internal raised panel > Image > Crop to Selection.
5. File > **Save as** > provide a name and browse the location you where you want to save.
6. Open the **Materials** window.
7. Click the drop-down menu > New Texture.
8. **Browse** for the saved image. **Open**.
9. **Type** a name in the material name field as Cherry Natural.
10. **Unlock** the aspect ratio keychain and modify the width to 12" and height to 3'-6".
11. Click on the **OK** button. The new texture will be incorporated to the **In Model** window.
12. If you want to save it for future use, proceed as explained in item 2.1
13. **Double-click** each group and apply the material on the rest of areas not yet painted.

Note: For the crown molding you can avoid editing the group and apply the texture to the closed group. Note here that the grain of the wood was set vertically and shall be applied so to the crown molding. If you want to be thorough instead of applying the texture to the closed group you should enter the edit mode, apply the material on one face, use the green pin to rotate the texture 90 degrees and then use the blue pin to conceal the edges of clearings dark image. You can sample the modified texture with Paint Bucket tool + Alt and then apply the material to the rest of the faces with Paint Bucket tool + Shift key. You could also rotate the image that serves as a reference for the texture in your editor and save it there as a new image. In that case in SketchUp change the texture image to your new one.

By using the plugin **Make Unique Texture ++** by Aerilius you can avoid most all the previous steps. The plugin offers two options. **Crop texture to selection** creates one new texture. **Make selected face(s) unique** creates for each selected face its own unique texture with best-fitting bounding box and bakes the UV distortion into it.

By using the plugin ThruPaint by Fredo you can apply the material to a closed group. ThruPaint resides within a suite of tools that Fredo calls FredoTools. This toolset is available for free on the SketchUcation forums. With this plugin you can choose different textures transformations such as rotation, mirror, or tiling. On Mac, you CANNOT use the native Material Selector because the Ruby API does not see the current material until it is applied with the native SU Paint tool. So you need to cycle through the model materials using the small arrows in the palette or TAB / Shift TAB. You can also sample the material from the model.

Complete the exercise by applying your chosen textures to the floor, countertop, backsplash and walls following the knowledge you have acquired.

3

Plugins and Dynamic Components to customize your design

This chapter will cover the use of some plugins and dynamic components available for the creation of kitchen cabinets. You can use the plugins to extend the functionality of SketchUp by making it more compatible with your needs. In any case throughout this book you can find various methods for designing kitchens where each is not exclusive of the others but can be combined for maximum productivity. The plugins used in this chapter are: Cab by T. Track, Cabinet by T. Burch, Kitchen by R. Wilson, Update Attributes Multiple DC, Replace Library DC all these three by SketchData and Product Connect by Igloo Studios. If you want to create your own library of cabinets a good alternative is to use one of these plugins to begin with. They can save you precious time.

To install plugins save the scripts in:
Windows: C:/program files/Google/SketchUp/Plugins
Mac: Library/Application Support/SketchUp 8/Plugins. Take note of the correct path for Mac; otherwise you will not able to see the plugin inside SketchUp. Once you have the plugin placed in the appropriate folder, you will need to restart SketchUp to activate the plugin. After you restart the program, if you don't see a Plugins tab in the menu bar, you might need to go to Preferences > Extensions > and turn on all of the extensions to activate the plugins menu.

The installation of a script into the plugins folder does not necessarily imply that the application will appear in the Plugins menu inside SketchUp. The author of the plugin can decide where in the menu will appear. For this reason, if after installing a plugin it does not appear in the Plugins menu look into the other menus.

Content

3.1 Cab by T. Track

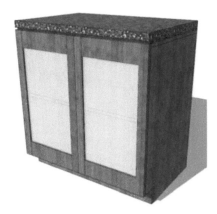

Cab.rb can be downloaded from the Ruby Library Depot (http://rhin.crai.archi.fr/rld/plugins_list_az.php) searching by name or under the author's name.

Place the file inside the plugins folder of SketchUp program. Open SketchUp. The plugin will be included in your menu automatically.

Details

1. Once you have installed cab.rb **open** SketchUp.
2. Open the **Plugins** menu > Cab.
3. Proceed to enter dimensions.
4. You will be prompted in a second dialogue box for the **door** dimensions. Enter dimensions.
5. You will be prompted in a third dialogue box for the **countertop** dimensions.

The component will be located at the origin. You may make modifications, erase faces, scale it or move it. If you want to skip the creation of the doors, enter in the dialogue box zero values.

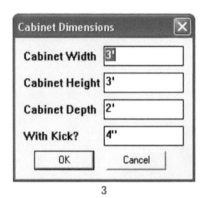

Cabinet Dimensions

Cabinet Width 3'
Cabinet Height 3'
Cabinet Depth 2'
With Kick? 4"

OK   Cancel

3

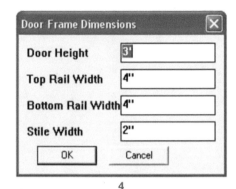

Door Frame Dimensions

Door Height 3'
Top Rail Width 4"
Bottom Rail Width 4"
Stile Width 2"

OK   Cancel

4

Countertop Optional

Counter Top Height 3'
Thickness 2"
Reveal 1/2"

OK   Cancel

5

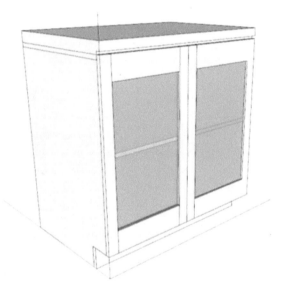

3.2   Working with Layers using Cabinet Plugin by T.Burch and Dynamic Components

Cabinet.rb can be downloaded from the Ruby Library Depot searching by name or under the author's name. Place the file inside the plugins folder of SketchUp program. Open SketchUp. The plugin will be included in your menu automatically.

Even though this cabinet does not include a door you can create the doors and insert them as separate components. In this exercise you will use a Dynamic Component and practice how to use layers with components to control visibility. You can use this method to show several alternatives of your project, inserting texts and dimensions that can be toggled off or on, or for any other use that requires controlling visibility of any object.

When you are structuring your model, keep in mind how you will present it, and how you plan to use scenes, groups, components and layers as anticipated in chapter 1. Specifically you need to think what entities in your model you might want to hide in particular scenes; to achieve this you will need to work with Layers.

In this example the scenes will show different groups assigned to different layers. You will turn on or off the appropriate layer before creating a scene (or updating it). This procedure will work even if the objects, in this case cabinet doors, are nested into a group like the RaiseCabinet group. This way you can have the benefit of nested groups in the Outliner, allowing you to hide cabinets while editing other parts of your model, but still have scenes that work. The lesson of this exercise is to use the Outliner as well as layers to give you the flexibility to use scenes effectively.

Details

1. Once you have installed cabinet.rb as explained before **open** SketchUp.
2. Open the **Camera** menu > **Cabinet Base**. (As said sometimes plugins install in different menus than Plugins)
3. Proceed to accept the default dimensions for the cabinet.
4. You will be prompt in a second dialogue box for the face frame dimensions. **Enter** default dimensions.
5. As a component is created, **double-click** to enter to the edit mode. Shorten the stiles and bring the sides back to create the toe kick. **Close** the component.

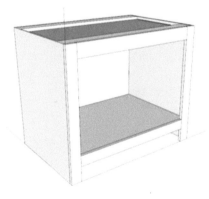

For the door you will use a dynamic component developed by Eric. To further explore the options offered by this dynamic component you can watch a video on http://SketchUptraining.blogspot.com/2009/06/using-dynamic-door.html

In this exercise, the attention will focus on how to combine scenes and layers to present different options with a single click.

6. **Open** your Component window and type in the search box "Dynamic Door by Eric". **Download** it into your model and place it in the correct position by rotating it along the blue axis.

7. Use the **Move** tool to move the door taking as initial reference the lower left endpoint of the outer frame. This frame is a guide to the proper location on the cabinet and in this particular case you are going to use an overlay door.

8. Once you have moved the cabinet door activate the Scale tool and modify the dimension to cover the front half of the cabinet and adjusting the height.

9. **Copy** the door by grabbing it from the exterior box and placing it on the other side of the cabinet. Do not worry if the two doors are not butted.

6

7

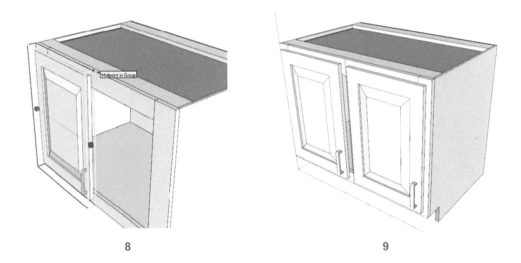

8   9

10. Select the right door > Right-Click > **Flip Along** > Component's Green to change the handle to the left.

11. **Repeat** the same step for both doors but this time flip along the blue axis to achieve the result shown in image 10-11.

12. Select both doors, and right-click > Dynamic Components > **Component options** > change Reveal to 0.25", ButtDoors, and Gap between Butt Doors to 0.125" > Apply.

13. **Copy** the two doors beside the cabinet.

14. Change the component options as in step 12 to Flat inside the PanelType drop-down menu. Change PullType to Knob.

10-11   14

15. **Create two groups**, one containing both raised doors and another one with the flat doors. Rename both groups inside the Outliner as shown.

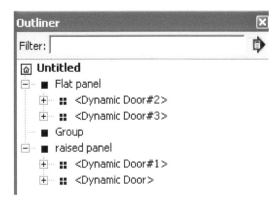

16. Open the **Layers** window and create two layers, one named Raised and the other Flat.

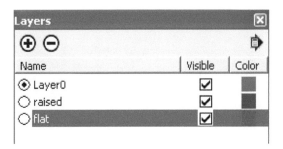

17. Select the "Raised" group, right-click > **Entity Info** > change the layer to Raised. Repeat the same steps for the flat panel doors placing them in layer Flat.
18. Turn the Flat layer off and open the **Scene** window. Create a scene and rename it "Raised panel".
19. Return to the **Layers** window and turn off the "Raised" layer and turn on "Flat" layer.
20. **Select** the flat doors group and **move** it to the correct position in front of the cabinet.
21. Create a **new scene** this time named "Flat panel".
22. Now you can select any scene and you will switch between the two cabinet options.
23. **Return** to the scene "Raised panel" and copy the cabinet and the doors twice.
24. **Select** the Flat panel scene. Note that when you copy a cabinet door type you are copying only one instance unless you turn on all layers first. If you select in the scene where the raised panel door is visible you are just selecting that group.

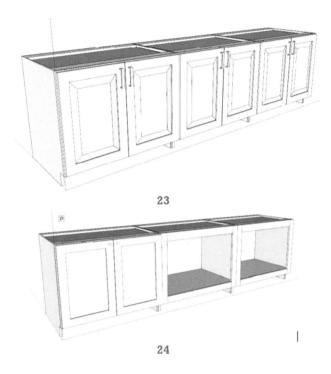

23

24

25. **Undo** the Copy step to regain a single cabinet.
26. To maintain the ability to switch the type of doors you should first put all the layers visible. Open the **layers** window, check all the layers, select with a crossing window and **copy** all the elements. Switch scenes to check the result.
27. Finally type in the Components window "Countertop Dynamic by Google". With this dynamic component you have the alternative of creating a straight, L-shaped or U-shaped, and also change materials. You can also use the scale tool to adjust them to your project dimension. On your own change the options to a straight countertop and apply any material of your choice using the Component Options window. In case you want to change the length of the countertop you can use the Scale tool applying the correspondent grip, and then retyping in the Measure toolbar the final dimension > enter.
28. Save as Kitchen3.2.

3.3 Inserting Wall Cabinets with Kitchen Plugin by R.Wilson

Kitchen.rb can be downloaded from the Ruby Library Depot searching by name or under the author's name. Place the file inside the plugins folder of SketchUp program. Open SketchUp. The plugin will be included in your menu automatically under the Draw menu with the name TOP_kitchen.

Even though this cabinet does not include a door, you can use the same type of doors used in the previous exercise.

Details

1. Once you have installed Kitchen.rb **open** SketchUp and open Kitchen3.2.
2. Check that you are in layer 0 while you perform this step. Open the **Draw** menu > **TOP_Kitchen**.

3. Change the Long field to 3' and Span to 48" (if you accepted the height of 2'-6" in item 3.2) and leave the others to the default dimensions. Span corresponds to the height from floor to bottom of the cabinet.

4. **Move** the cabinet backward to align it with the back of the base cabinets.

5. Open the **Outliner** and rename the wall cabinet. Since you have not renamed the base cabinets yet click on each word "Group" to highlight it. A blue bounding box will show in the model corresponding with the chosen word. Right-click > **Rename** > base cabinet for those

correspondent. Repeat with the wall cabinet. Your Outliner should show something similar to this picture.

6. **Copy** a raised panel group and place it on the wall cabinet. Be aware to select the group from the back left endpoint of the outside box to be able to place it in the correct position on the wall cabinet.

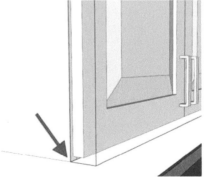

7. **Scale** the group to adjust height.
   If cabinet door disappears open the outliner and unhide all the hidden components.

8. Select the raised doors. Right-click > **Flip Along** > Group's Blue. Scale them.

9. Select the wall cabinet and doors and create two copies to the right.

10. Click on **scene** Flat panels. At this point you will notice that no doors are showing on the wall cabinets.
11. Copy one group of flat doors from the base cabinets and place it on top of the left wall cabinet.

12. **Scale** the group to match the wall cabinet height.
13. **Copy** the scaled group two more times for each wall cabinet.
14. **Select** the three groups of doors and flip along the blue direction to place the handle correctly.

15. You can use the **Paint Bucket** tool to apply any color that you want.
16. Save it.

3.4 Inserting Dynamic Components and changing attributes of many components at the same time

In the following exercise you will use a sink that mounts itself into the countertop. You will also insert dynamic components developed by SketchData, and then select multiple components to change the attributes in a single step. In SketchUp each component must be individually selected to change its attributes.

SketchData has developed a plugin that lets you select multiple components at once and change the attributes in a single step. These plugins save time when you may need to change dimensions or cabinet pulls. Before starting the next exercise you will need to install the plugins. To do it so visit http://www.sketchdata.com/ > Downloads > Download inside the plugins folder of SketchUp "Replace Library Dynamic Components Plug-in" and "Update Dynamic Component Attributes". Unzip the file. To complete the installation of "Replace Library Dynamic Component Plugin" move the SketchData Cabinet Pulls folder inside the SketchUp/Components folder. Open the program. Check the installation on the Plugins menu under SketchData.

This exercise will also teach you how to add favorite libraries in the Components window to avoid searching the same model in the 3DWarehouse at a later time. SketchData has a big variety of generic dynamic components that can be modified through a diverse variety of attributes.

Details

1. Download from the 3D Warehouse "Kitchen3.4 by agra" and open as a new file.
2. Type "Cabinets Frameless Dynamic Components by Sketchdata" in the Components window. Since you will be working with various components of this collection you will include it as favorite collection on the components window.
3. Click on the Details button of the components window and select "**Add to favorites**". Click on the navigation arrow ▼ to verify that SketchData collection was added to the list. This is the same way you can include libraries of any manufacturer.
4. Click on the link Cabinet – Wall and select the W1UD component. Place it on the wall next to the tall cabinet.
5. Right-click > Dynamic Components > **Component Options** > change parameters 14"H x 36"W x 14"D.
6. **Copy** the same component below the previous one this time changing the attributes to 16"H. Reposition the two cabinets again matching the cabinets' height.

4-5-6

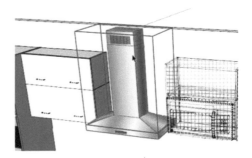

7

7. Select View menu > **Hidden Geometry**. Select the hood mesh > right-click > **Unhide**. This is another way to select geometry without searching through the Outliner.
8. **Uncheck** Hidden Geometry from the View menu.
9. Type W0DMW in the components window. Download the file into your model. Change attributes as shown. Place it beside the hood aligning it with the rest of the cabinets.

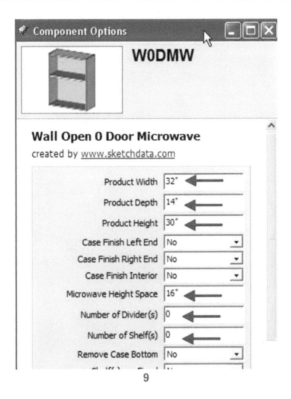

9

10. Open the Components window and type JVM1850SMSS GE. Select the Spacemaker® Over-the-Range Microwave Oven. Insert it inside the lower shelf. You can activate the X-Ray face style mode to help yourself position it.
11. **Copy** the W1UD component to the right and change attributes as shown in the picture below. Be aware of the correct position so all cabinets are aligned.

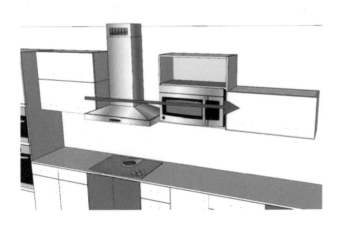

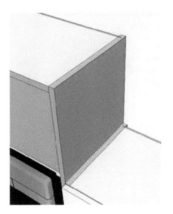

11   11

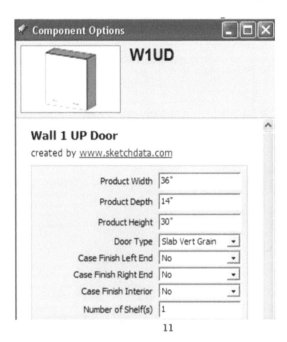

11

12. **Copy** one more time W1UD component to the right and change width attributes to 24".

13. **Type** W0D in the components window. Place it in the corner, change attributes to:

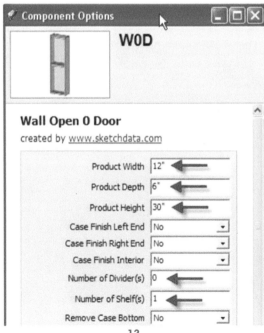

13

14. **Type** Wfiller in the components window. Place it in the corner and change attributes to:

14

SketchThis.net has modeled a number of sinks to place on countertops. They will automatically make the cut on the face. However, to get positive results you should not insert them within a group or component. In the present exercise the countertop has not been grouped. After the sink and faucet insertion you can select all elements and group them. Remember to rename it inside the Outliner.

15. **Type** "dynamic sink by Erik" in the search box of the Components window. Add them as favorites.
16. **Select** Artisan AR3218-D10_8. Place it on top of the countertop face. Move it so it is aligned with the midpoint of base cabinet.

17. Select from the **3D Warehouse** "Pilar Touch 4380T" faucet and insert it centering with the sink.

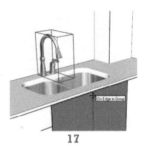

17

18. **Orbit** around to see the back of the island.
19. Select the **Section Plane** tool and place it on the back wall. Move it forward to have a complete view of the island.

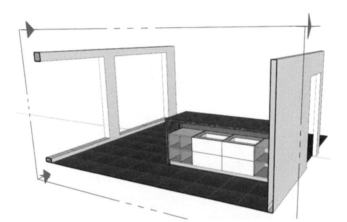

20. Click on the Display Section Planes icon to hide the section plane.

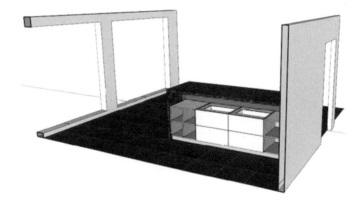

21. Select the four cabinets under the island countertop. **Plugins** menu > SketchData > **Attribute update (simple)**. Type in the Product Height field under the Value column 41". Click on the apply button. After a few seconds the four cabinets will be updated to the new dimension. The difference between Simple and Complex plugins is basically the level of detail. While the Simple shows only the first instance of attributes, Complex shows all the levels.

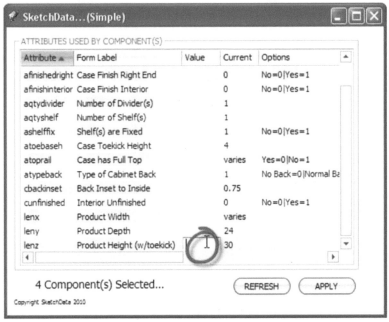

21

22. **Double-click** on drawer handle until you reach the handle level. Select it.

23. Right-click > **Replace Library Dynamic Component**. If you do not have this option you probably missed something when you installed the plugin and you should verify your steps.

24. Open the SketchData folder and choose HDW_Pull_BP19541 or any other that you like. Reply "Yes" to the prompt of replacing all components. Close group.

25. Turn off Display Section Cuts. Orbit to face the wall cabinets. Notice that drawers changed handles while cabinet doors remained the same. This is because each collection belongs to a different category so in that way you can control the type of handles and their position for drawers, tall cabinets, wall cabinets, etc.

26. Repeat the last step to change the cabinet handles.

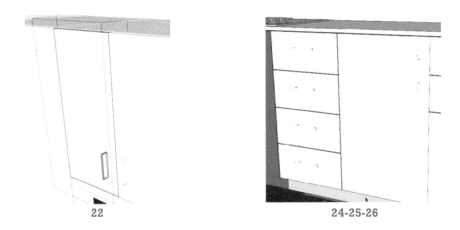

22   24-25-26

27. On your own create different scenes with elevations and save the file.

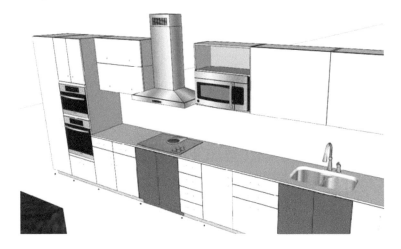

Note: This plugin can be used with any components that you have saved in your hard drive.

3.5   Product Connect by Igloo

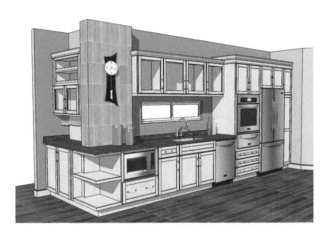

Another plugin that was launched is Product Connect by Igloo. The plugin is designed to help you get more out of models stored in the 3D Warehouse. The key is that the 3D models must be enabled to work with this application to take advantage of all the benefits of the plugin. Product Connect enabled 3D models are rich with information like codes, website links, and dimensions. The Report Maker tool formats all the information into a product schedule. A recent addition includes some features that allow you to make reports with any other product out of Product Connect collection.

After adding these models to your SketchUp project, you can use the Product Connect plugin to export the data as a spreadsheet. You can find a full list of compatible models in the Product Connect collection of the 3D Warehouse. Type Product Connect and then sort by collections. At the time this book was written 25 manufacturers collections were included.

Even though the plugin is free you need to register in Igloo website in order to access to the download page. After downloading, execute the file. This step will install the plugin inside SketchUp. Product Connect features three main tools that help you create product reports from within SketchUp:

•**Report Maker** displays preview information about products in a SketchUp model.
•**Product Editor** is a new tool that allows you to turn any component or material into a product that can be included in reports created using Report Maker.
•**Get Products** is a tool that helps you find and download Product Connect compatible products from the 3D Warehouse.

In this exercise you will use a model from Igloo gallery to try this plugin.

Details

1. Register and install the plugin from www.igloostudios.com.
2. Open a new file. Select File menu > 3D Warehouse > **Get Model**. Type "Portrait Kitchen Vignette".
3. Select "Portrait Kitchen Vignette by Merillat" and download it into your model.
4. Open Plugins menu > Product Connect > **Report Maker** or use the icon.
5. Select a product schedule type such as Cabinet or Appliance. A window appears showing the collected data.

6. Click the **Create Reports** button. The plugin generates a spreadsheet containing all of the product models as well as their relevant data that is saved in the same location where your SU model is saved.

7. Another feature of this plugin is to report on material textures that have been applied to faces inside of a <u>component</u>.

8. Type in your component window "Formica 180fx". This is a Product Connect enabled collection. Select any thumbnail and download it into your model.

9. **Double-click** the 3D model to enter to the edit mode until you reach the countertop instance.

10. Click on the **Paint Bucket** tool. Open your **In Model** materials window or sample any swatch Alt/Opt key.

11. Apply the chosen Formica material to the countertop. Close Group.

12. Open the **Outliner**. Double-click your model again to enter to the edit mode. Select the countertop group. The group will be highlighted inside the Outliner. Right-click > **Make component** > Rename it "Countertop".

Note: Report Maker is able to identify only compatible materials that are applied to faces within components. Materials inside of groups and/or "Loose" faces will not show up in a report.

13. **Delete** the material samples that you downloaded from the 3D Warehouse.

14. **Save** your file.

15. Run **Report Maker** .

16. Select **Finish** as Product Schedule type.

17. To know the area of the countertop double-click until you reach the face instance. Select **View** menu > **Hidden Geometry** to allow selecting the geometry > right-click > Entity Info > read the value in the Area box. You can transfer this information to the product schedule.

2 Review component list:

Schedule	Manufacturer	Product Number	Product Name
Finish	Formica		Standard Laminate 180fx® - Burnished Montana 3471

18. Download a cabinet from the Sketchdata collection saved already in Favorites.

19. Select the component and choose Plugins menu > Product Connect > Product Editor.

20. Click on the value "none" beside Product name. Add information.
21. Purge unused components to avoid any duplication.
22. Run Report Maker again.
23. Select only the Sketchdata cabinet. Run Report Maker; it will only include the selected component.

4

How to create Dynamic Components

Any model you create can be a component and any component can potentially be a Dynamic Component. As you have seen through this book Dynamic Components have parametric attributes such as a cabinet component that can be resized or whose doors can open and close. Items such as the component's name, description, size, and material, are attributes. Some of them are predefined attributes, available for every dynamic component. Conversely, custom attributes are unique attributes defined by the developer of the dynamic component.

Every component attribute has a value which can be a textual string, a number, or the result of a formula. For example, the attribute called "Name" might have the value of "Cabinet Single Door" or the length attribute called "LenX" might have the value of 32". Formulas can consist of predefined functions, mathematical operators, or the values of other attributes. You can refer to Functions as shortcuts that perform some operation, such as calculating the square root of a number.
Refer to http://SketchUp.google.com/support/bin/answer.py?answer=114561 to learn more about the supported functions.

All SketchUp users can use dynamic components. However, only SketchUp Pro users can develop dynamic components. Dynamic components will have an icon ⇒ on its thumbnail when it meets all the criteria to be considered one. Common features of Dynamic Components are "Constrained" "Configurable" or "Branded". For example, a dynamic cabinet door component might have a frame of a set size such as 3" or can have a pre-defined set of values that are configurable by the user or can include product and company information, such as contact information, product details, and links to a product web site.

Given the vast repertoire of attributes that can be defined in a Dynamic Component you will limit the following exercise to defining different sizes, materials, prices, changes of position of the handle located on the right or left of the door, repeating a sub-component, and setting to use the Interact tool.

Content

4.1   How to create a dynamic cabinet

To create a dynamic component the first step that you need to do is to create a component to which you will later give some attributes. In the first steps you will use the cabinet plugin explained in item 3.2 of the previous chapter.

Details

1. Open a new file. Camera > **Cabinet Base** > Change the width to 2' and leave the rest of default parameters. Enter into the edit mode to change the toe kick as shown in the picture.
2. Draw on the front of the cabinet the door using the **Rectangle** tool and the **Push/Pull** tool. You may even include reveals to hide the back box in case it has a different material.
3. **Select** the door entities and **create a component**. Name it as Cabinet Door.

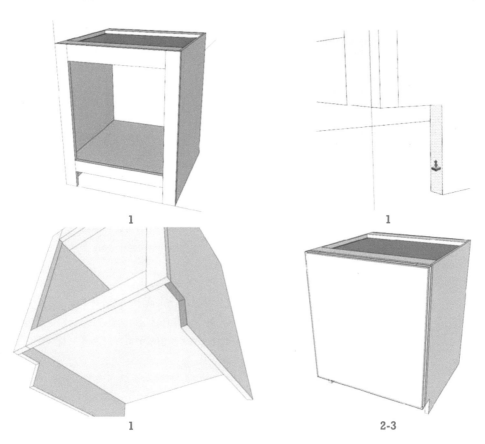

1

1

1

2-3

4. Type **HDW_PULL_BP** in the Component window search field. **Download** it. With the **Move** tool rotate it 90 degrees and place it at 1.5" from the edge of the door on the right side. Right-click>Dynamic Components > **Component Options** > Change the pull length to 100 mm.

5. Open the **Outliner** and rename the "Group" as "Box". **Erase** any guidelines that you have drawn to place the handle. Select the two components and the group and make a new component named "Base Cabinet Single Door".

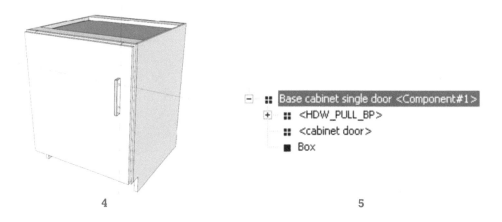

4   5

Once you have done your component you have to create your dynamic component by accessing the Component Attributes menu.

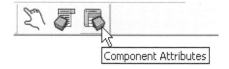

You can also right-click on top of the component > Dynamic Components > Component Attributes. You will then have predetermined and custom options to add.

6. To add a predefined attribute click on the **Add attribute** button in the Component Attributes dialogue box under Base Cabinet Single Door section. A list of predefined attributes appears. A field with the phrase 'Enter Name' also appears.

7. Click on **Position** attribute. The name appears in the first column of the Component Attributes dialogue box. By changing the values of any of the three axes with an"=" sign on the front will constrain the position of your component to those coordinates. Since you are going to use this cabinet in different locations and positions do not change any values. To change a value in any field you can double-click on the field to access to the edit mode.

8. Click  to add **Size** as a new predetermined attribute. Again, if you change any of the values with an = sign on the front you will constrain the dimension of the cabinet to that size. These means that if you scale the component or use any other tool that implies a size change once you redraw the element it will recover the original size. Redrawing can be done in many ways, for example by moving or by right-click > Dynamic Components > Redraw.

9. Click once on LenX and click the **Detail** icon on the side of the attribute to predetermine a list of different width options.

10. Change the Display rule to "**Users can select from a list**". Type the custom name that you want to appear when you are entering values in your Component Options dialogue menu. In this case type "**Width**".

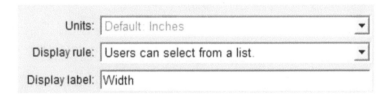

11. Click on the **Add option** button and create your list option as shown.

List Option	Value
24"	24"
28"	28"
30"	30"
32"	32"
⊕ Add option	

12. Click the **Apply** button.

13. To see the results open the Component Options 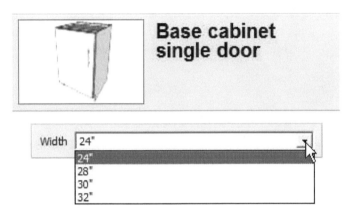 menu. You will have a drop-down menu with your different size options. By selecting any option within the list and clicking on the **Apply** button your component will be resized to the new attribute value.

14. **Save**.

Base cabinet single door

Width	24"
	24"
	28"
	30"
	32"

4.2 How to create a list of different materials options in a dynamic component

You can also define materials to be applied to the faces. Materials to apply must be within the model file. To ensure that the selection of materials accompany the component a good technique is to embed a swatch of the materials as a subcomponent of the main component. In this way the materials are loaded into the In Model library; otherwise the material will not be found when you intend to apply it. To show you this procedure type "cabinet material swatch by agra" in your component window. Download the swatch into your model.

Details

1. To embed the swatch in your component a good practice is to locate it inside the component in a place where is not noticeable. Orbit around and place it under the bottom of the cabinet. Scale the swatch to diminish its size.
2. Open the **Outliner** and **drag** the swatch inside the cabinet component. Select the word again > right-click > Hide the swatch.

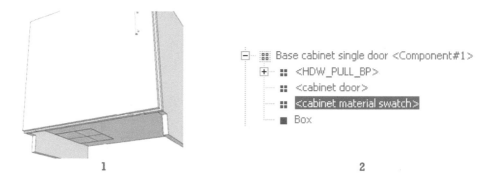

1   2

3. Once you have included the materials in your component you will need to add the material attribute to the DC. Click the **Add attribute** button in the Base Cabinet Single Door section of the Component Attributes window > choose **Material** under the Behaviors section.
4. Click the **Detail** icon on the side of the attribute.
5. Change the Display rule to "**Users can select from a list**". **Type** as custom name "Material".
6. Click on the **Add option** button and create your list option as shown. The value for each color is the name of the material that appears in the Materials window when you select a thumbnail.

List Option	Value
White	Color_000
Wood	Wood_Cherry_Original
OSB	Wood_OSB
Raised panel	panel1
⊕ Add option	

7. Click the **Apply** button.
8. Open your **Component Options** window and choose any material from the drop-down menu. **Apply**.

When designing cabinets you may wish to apply different materials to different components within a model. In this case you will need to include the material attribute to each subcomponent while you create a custom attribute for the cabinet itself.

9. **Click** ⊕ *Add attribute* in the Cabinet Single Door section of the Component Attributes window to add a Custom name as a new attribute. **Type** "Box" where "Enter Name" reads > Enter > click on the **Detail** icon. Create a new list as shown and apply.

Users can select from a list.

Box material

List Option	Value
OSB	Wood_OSB
White	Color_000
Wood	Wood_Cherry_Original
⊕ Add option	

9

Custom

| ⊖ | Box | Color_000 | ⇨ |
| ⊕ | Add attribute | | |

⊞ **HDW_DBAR** inch

⊞ **Box** inch

9

10. Click on the (**+**) sign beside Box section to expand it > **Add attribute** > Behaviors > **Material**.

11. **Type** "**=**" and then **point with the mouse** to the Box word in the Base cabinet single door section. By doing this you are selecting the same type of attribute without having to type it again linking both sections. Enter.

12. To finish, open the **Component Options** and choose a material for the box and another for the rest.

13. **Save**.

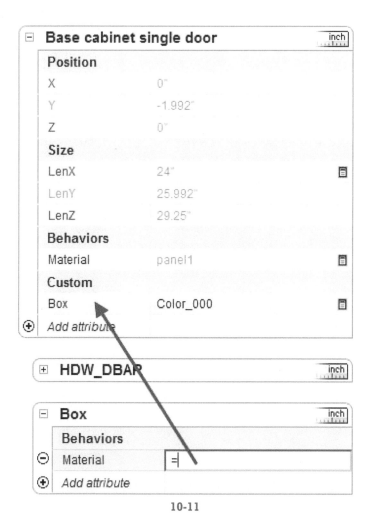

10-11

Note the link chain starting from parents to children attributes to keep consistency in the formulas.

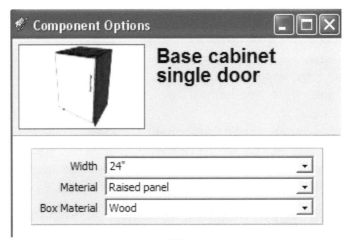

12

Note: In case you have chosen the raised panel in the Material section the image position might not be correct, especially when you change cabinet size. In that case, edit the material inside the In Model 🏠 *Material window to adjust size or color.*

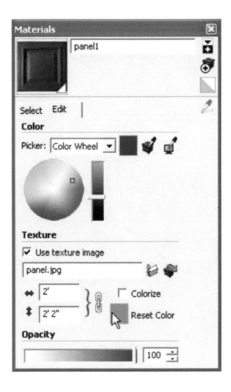

4.3 How to use a logical function to change the handle hand side

In this exercise you will learn to apply a logic function to define the placement of the handle to a left-handed door or right-handed door. You will use the function "IF" which identifies a logical test. The test argument is any value or expression that can be TRUE or FALSE. The thenValue (optional) is the value that is returned if the logical test is TRUE. The elseValue (optional) is the value that is returned if the logical test is FALSE.

All the attributes you want to be visible or have interaction with the user should be included in the first level of the hierarchical tree. These options will show when you open Components Option window, in this particular case "Base Cabinet Single Door". Beside these attributes you must define the variables that will give a value to the "right" and "left" position. Once defined these variables are the argument of the logic function that will do the test to make it true or false.

The handle that you have downloaded from the 3DWarehouse already contains arguments of Dynamic Components (DC) which you will leave intact and you will add just a few more. In a later exercise you will learn how to animate a swing door. The Position attribute can be applied in different ways with shelves, handles or drawers.

Details

The first step is to include a Door Hand list where the user can choose the left or right side option.

1. **Add attribute** in the Base Cabinet Single Door section defined as "DoorHand" > Enter.
2. Click on the **Details** button. Write the Display Label and select the values for Right and Left, in this case numbers 1 and 2. Apply.

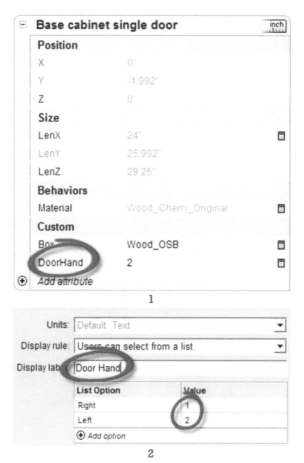

1

2

The second step is to define the variable "left" and "right" since the position of the handle will vary accordingly. Note that you already have width variables that change the size of the cabinet but the handle should be placed at the same distance from the edge no matter if you change the width of the cabinet.

3. **Expand** the "Cabinet Door" section and **add** two attributes that will define the position of the handle for both options; named them "Lhand" and "Rhand". The value for Lhand will be the width of the cabinet (variable) minus 1.5". The Rhand value will be width of the cabinet minus the width of the cabinet + 1.5" (these are the distances to the origin). For Lhand type (=) sign and then point with the mouse to field LenX of the Base Cabinet Single Door, type "-1.5" > Enter. For Rhand type (=) sign and then point with the mouse to field LenX of the Base Cabinet Single Door > type (-) sign and then point with the mouse to field LenX of the Base Cabinet Single Door > type "+1.5" > Enter. You can select the Toggle Formula Button ![=fx] to see the formula instead of numbers.

The third step is to define the logical function to constrain the handle position when the option right or left is chosen.

4. **Expand** the HDW_DBAR section. Click on the X of the Position section and type "**=IF**(point with the mouse to the DoorHand value in the Cabinet Single Door section, > type "**=1**," point with the mouse to Rhand of the cabinet door section, > type "**,**" and finally > point with the mouse the Lhand value > close brackets. If a red tag is indicating Parens count it means that you made a mistake in some part of the formula.

5. Open the **Components Option** window and toggle between right and left to check functionality changing cabinet's sizes. **Save**.

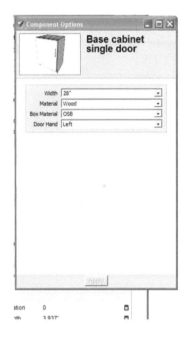

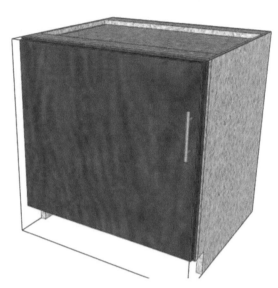

4.4   How to implement dynamic pricing

You can create a component whose pricing changes based on the type of material or size of component the user chooses.

Details

1. Open the **Components Attributes** window at the top-level component "Base Cabinet Single Door".
2. Click on the **Add Attribute** button > **Type** "Cost" and press the **Tab** key. The attribute named "Cost" is placed in the list of attributes called "Custom". The field next to the Cost attribute is opened for editing.

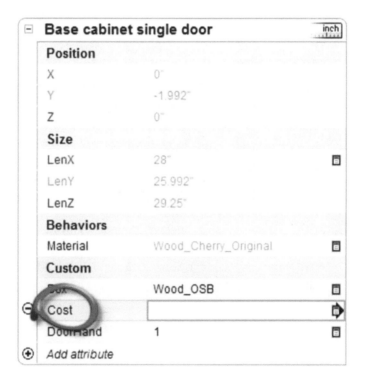

3. **Type:**
   =IF(Material="Color_000",$80,If(Material="Wood_Cherry_Original",$10 0,IF(Material="Wood_OSB",$60,IF(Material="panel1",$120)))).

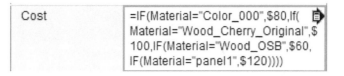

4. Press the **Enter** key to accept the formula. This formula assigns a cost for the cabinet based on the material that is selected by the user. Be careful to type the name of the materials exactly the way they are called in the Materials window, including lower or upper case.

5. Click on the **Detail** button. Change the profile of the Cost attribute as shown.

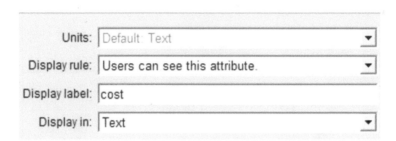

6. **Save**

7. Following the same idea you can combine the **IF** and **AND** logical functions to combine material, size, and pricing. Note that in the formula below there were only assigned price differentiation for Color_000 and Wood_Cherry_Original while Wood_OSB and panel1 only have one price no matter the size.

    =IF(AND(Material="Color_000",LenX=24),$80,
    IF(AND(Material="Color_000",LenX=28),$85,
    IF(AND(Material="Color_000",LenX=30),$90,
    IF(AND(Material="Color_000",LenX=32),$95,
    IF(AND(Material="Wood_Cherry_Original",LenX=24),$100,
    IF(AND(Material="Wood_Cherry_Original",LenX=28),$105,
    IF(AND(Material="Wood_Cherry_Original",LenX=30),$110,
    IF(AND(Material="Wood_Cherry_Original",LenX=32),$115,
    IF(Material="Wood_OSB",$60,IF(Material="panel1",$120,$60)))))))))))

4.5 How to repeat a sub-component like a shelf and adjust the spacing in between

A repetitive dynamic component is a component containing a sub-component that is able to repeat, such as shelves of a cabinet. In this exercise you are going to replicate the shelf sub-component as the component is scaled in the X and Z direction. The main issue when creating a repeated sub-component is the spacing between each replicated part and how the part is replicated. By now your component attributes hierarchy tree should look similar to this picture:

The first step you will do is to create the shelf as a new component and then insert it inside the cabinet as a sub-component. In this example, the shelf is an inch smaller on each side of the cabinet. Obviously these dimensions are variable and will depend on the thickness of each of the parts of the cabinet, but for the sake of this exercise you will work with preset dimensions. The shelves must have attributes that allow them to grow in length when you specify different widths of the cabinet and at the same time they can be replicated in height when you specify the number of shelves.

Details

1. **Draw** a rectangle on top of the cabinet and then allow a ¾" of thickness with the **Pull/Push** tool. After this step select the shelf entities and create a component. Name it "Shelf".
2. Open the **Outliner** and drag the shelf inside the cabinet. Shelf will appear in your Component Attributes window as part of your cabinet.

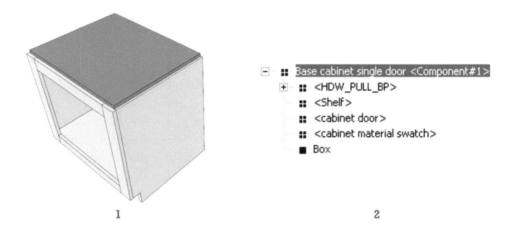

1   2

3. **Add** a new **attribute** in the Base Cabinet Single Door section > Enter name "QtShelf" > Click the **Detail** button > Write and choose the shown settings > **Apply**. A new field will show in the Component Option window. Write "1" in the Quantity of Shelf(s) field.

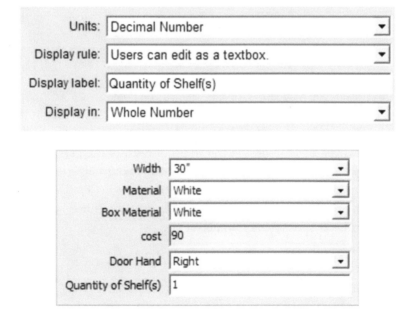

4. Return to the **Component Attributes** window and expand the Box section > **Add Attribute** > Enter name "BtmHgt" to define the lower Z height at the shelf should be. This value can be a variable or a prefixed number. In this exercise you will constrain the height to 5.38" > Type *"=5.38"*

5. Continue in the Box section of the Component Attributes window > **Add Attribute** > Enter name "TopHgt" to define the total thickness of the cabinet top. As the bottom value you will prefix a number. Type "=1".

6. Continue in the Box section of the Component Attributes window > **Add Attribute** > Enter name "InsideHgt" to define the total space you will have available to accommodate the shelves once they are placed. To define the value, enter (=) and point with your mouse to the LenZ field of the cabinet section > (-) sign > point the TopHgt cell. With this step you took away from the total height the top cabinet thickness. You will select the bottom height in another step.

7. Since the length of the shelves will vary according to the selected option in the Component Options window, you will need to link the length with the cabinet width options. Continue in the Box section of the Component Attributes window > **Add Attribute** > Enter name "Lside". Click on the value column and type **=1**.

8. Continue in the Box section of the Component Attributes window > **Add Attribute** > Enter name "Rside". Click on the value column and **type =1**.

⊟ **Box**	inch
Behaviors	
Material	=Base Cabinet Single Door!Box
Custom	
BtmHgt	=5.38"
InsideHgt	=Base Cabinet Single Door! LenZ-TopHgt
Lside	=1
Rside	=1
TopHgt	=1
⊕ *Add attribute*	

9. **Toggle** between formulas and values view by clicking on [=fx] button on the right top corner.

10. Open the Shelf section. Add **Position** and **Size** attributes to the list. Enter in the X value cell **=Box!Lside**. You can point with the mouse the Lside field of the Box section (refer to the pictures shown at the end of this chapter).

11. Click on the **Add Attribute** button and select from the Behaviors section **Material** > "**=**" > **Point** with the mouse the Material value field of the Box.

12. The next step is to define the spacing between the shelves according to the chosen quantities. Click on the **Add Attribute** and write "Spacing". Type **=Box!InsideHgt/Base Cabinet Single Door!QtShelf+1**. This formula will divide the inside height by the required spaces depending the quantity of shelves you enter in the Component Options window.

13. Click on the **Add Attribute** button. Click on the **Copies** attribute in the list. The field is populated with the word "Copies" and the field next to the "Copies" attribute is opened for editing. You need to create a formula that will yield a number of copies given the inside height of the cabinet. Type **=(Box!InsideHgt)/(LenZ+Spacing)**

14. The position in Z will vary according the quantity of shelves you specify in the Component options window. The value will be defined by the cabinet Z position plus the box bottom height plus the quantity of copies times their thickness. This formula uses a predefined attribute called 'Copy' to determine Z positioning for each shelf. The Copy attribute is simply a counter that begins at 0 (for the original shelf) and adds one for each additional copy. So, Copy is equal to 1 for the first copy, equal to 2 for the second copy, equal to 3 for the third copy, and so on. However, you will only ever see the Z value for the original shelf component in the Component Attributes dialogue box.
Type in the Z value **=Base cabinet single door!Z+Box!BtmHgt+(copy+1)*(Box!InsideHgt-((Copies+1)*LenZ))/(Copies+2)+copy*LenZ**

15. Type in the LenX value cell **=Base cabinet single door!LenX-Box!Lside-Box!Rside**. This formula will define the variable of the chosen width less the thickness of the left and right sides of the box.

16. Finally you will add the **Hidden** attribute under behavior. This attribute contains either a 1 (TRUE) to hide the component or 0 (FALSE) to unhide the component. After adding the attribute type in the value field **=IF(Base cabinet single door!QtShelf>0,FALSE,TRUE)**

17. **Close** the Component Attributes window and open the Component Options window

18. Open the View menu > Face Style > **X-ray**. Enter different numbers for quantity of shelves, check results. **Save**.

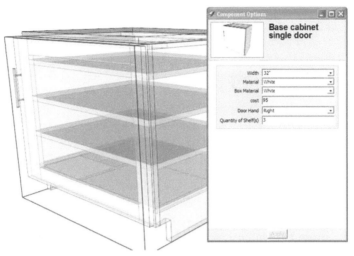

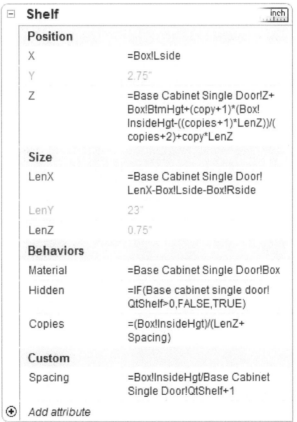

Shelf	inch
Position	
X	=Box!Lside
Y	2.75"
Z	=Base Cabinet Single Door!Z+Box!BtmHgt+(copy+1)*(Box!InsideHgt-((copies+1)*LenZ))/(copies+2)+copy*LenZ
Size	
LenX	=Base Cabinet Single Door!LenX-Box!Lside-Box!Rside
LenY	23"
LenZ	0.75"
Behaviors	
Material	=Base Cabinet Single Door!Box
Hidden	=IF(Base cabinet single door!QtShelf>0,FALSE,TRUE)
Copies	=(Box!InsideHgt)/(LenZ+Spacing)
Custom	
Spacing	=Box!InsideHgt/Base Cabinet Single Door!QtShelf+1
⊕ Add attribute	

Note: Text must always appear in quotes in a formula. The number sign (#) indicates an error in your formula. If a variable is included in a formula but it has yet not been created it will show as an error too.

4.6 How to animate a dynamic component

A dynamic component can have animated sub-components that move when the user clicks on the component with the Interaction tool. Animations can be used in components that have moving parts such as doors, drawers, and appliances. The animate function starts an animation that changes to subsequent values on successive clicks. After the last value the animation returns to the first state.

The value of the attribute will change to the next value in a list of parameters every half a second. For example, if the ONCLICK attribute contains ANIMATE("X",0,100), and the user clicks on the component, the component would animate the value of the "X" attribute between 0 and 100. A subsequent click would animate back to 0 from 100. If more than two animate states are passed, then the value will toggle between them in order. So, if the ONCLICK attribute equals ANIMATE("ROTZ",0,-130,10,100) the animation would go through each of the 4 values with each click.

This function animates with default easing. Easing is the speed of the animation (on a scale of 0 to 100, 0 being fastest). Easing is represented by two numbers; the first number (easein) identifies the speed at the start of the animation. The second number (easeout) identifies the speed at the end of the animation. Default easing is 0,100 (animation starts fast but slows down at the end).

Other considerations to take into account are that nesting a component (Child) within another component (Parent) upon which the ONCLICK attribute is being applied (as a door handle within a door panel) determines its position relative to the axis of the Parent component. So if the Parent rotates, the Child has to rotate as well. In the case of a door panel component and a handle component you will need to select both components and make a new one, called Cabinet Door, out of both of these. The Handle and Door Panel components are now nested into the Cabinet Door. If Door Panel rotates then the Handle will rotate as well.

In this exercise you will also discover how an animation varies according to the selection of the hand of a door. Because the position of the hinges changes the direction of rotation of the door, you will learn how to make a component that works for both ways.

Details

1. Select in the **Component Options** dialogue box the Left door hand.
2. Open the **Outliner** and **drag** Cabinet Door and HDW_PULL_BP outside the Base Cabinet Single Door DC.
3. **Explode** the Cabinet Door.
4. **Select** the door panel entities and HDW_PULL_BP and make a **copy** aside.
5. With the copy still selected > Right-click > **Flip Along** > Red Direction.

2   4

6. **Select** the door panel entities and handle on top of the cabinet box and create a component. Place the component axes in the bottom left back corner. Name it "DoorL". Note that the location of the component axes is important since they define the pivot rotation point.
7. **Select** the entities of other door > Right-click > **Make Component** > Name= DoorR > Set Component Axes > Change axes to the bottom right corner as shown in picture 7.
8. Select the DoorL > Right-click > Dynamic Components > **Component Attributes**.
9. Add attributes **RotZ** and **onClick**. Create a **custom attribute** named "Openness".
10. Enter "**0**" in the Openness value field.
11. Enter **=openness** in the RotZ value field.
12. Type **animate("openness",0,-110)** in the onClick value field.
13. **Select** the DoorR > Right-click > Dynamic Components > Component Attributes.
14. Add attributes **RotZ** and **onClick**. Create a **custom attribute** named Openness.
15. Enter "**0**" in the Openness value field.

16. Enter **=openness** in the RotZ value field.
17. Type **animate("openness",0,110)** in the onClick value field.

18. Click on the Interact with Dynamic Components icon 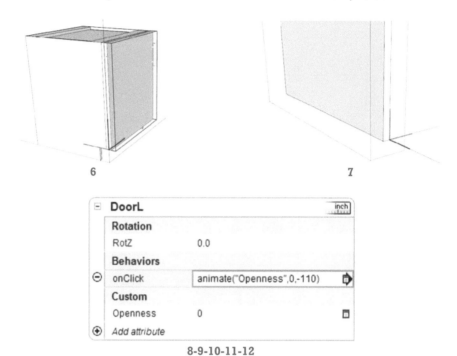 and check functionality on both doors and return to the closed position.

6   7

⊟ **DoorL**		inch
Rotation		
RotZ	0.0	
Behaviors		
⊖ onClick	animate("Openness",0,-110)	
Custom		
Openness	0	
⊕ Add attribute		

8-9-10-11-12

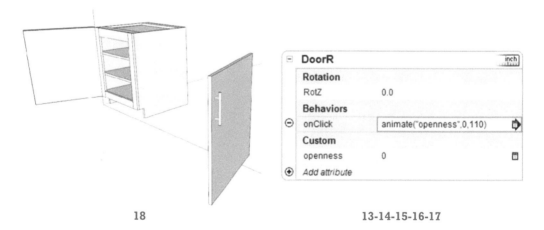

⊟ **DoorR**		inch
Rotation		
RotZ	0.0	
Behaviors		
⊖ onClick	animate("openness",0,110)	
Custom		
openness	0	
⊕ Add attribute		

18   13-14-15-16-17

19. **Move** DoorR on top of the DoorL matching the same position.
20. Select DoorL and DoorR in the **Outliner** and create a **new component**. Name it "Door". Accept the default settings.

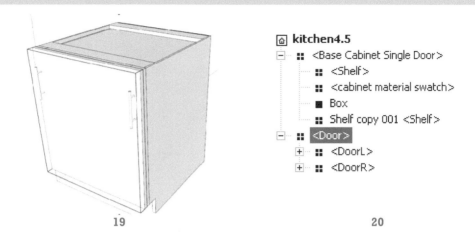

kitchen4.5
- :: <Base Cabinet Single Door>
  - :: <Shelf>
  - :: <cabinet material swatch>
  - ■ Box
  - :: Shelf copy 001 <Shelf>
  - :: <Door>
    - :: <DoorL>
    - :: <DoorR>

19   20

In the following steps you are going to incorporate the doors to the cabinet and make the doors open in the correct way as the door hand is selected in the Component Options window.

21. With the Door component selected click on the **Component Attributes** icon   .

22. Add to the Door section **Position** and **Size** attributes.

23. Click on the **Add attribute** button and type "aDoorHand". Do not enter any value yet.

24. Open the **Outliner** and **drag** the word Door below the Base Cabinet Single Door word to include the Door in the DC.

25. Select the Base Cabinet Single Door in the **Outliner** and open the **Attributes** window. Find the Door section and type in the aDoorHand value field *=Base Cabinet Single Door!DoorHand* (You can point with the mouse to create the link).

26. Select Door in the **Outliner** to access to DoorL and DoorR children attributes. Add to each subcomponent aDoorHand attribute entering in the value field *=Door!aDoorhand*

Note that along all the exercises you had to keep a link always starting from parents to children attributes to keep consistency in the formulas.

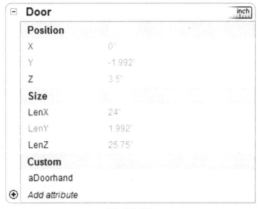

21-22-23

24

25

26

27. Still in the DoorL section add Hidden attribute. Type in the value field **=if(aDoorHand=1,1,0)** (You can point with the mouse to the aDoorHand field). This formula changes the variable that if the door is right-handed the left door component will hide.

28. Open DoorR section and add Hidden attribute. Type in the value field **=if(aDoorHand=1,0,1)** (You can point with the mouse to the aDoorHand field). This formula enter the variable that if the door is NOT right-handed the left door component will unhide.

29. Check functionality with the **Interact** tool.

27

28

Note: The procedures in this chapter are just a few guidelines on how to set up a dynamic component. Many companies and users of SketchUp with deep mathematical basis have enriched the 3D Warehouse saving valuable time for designers. Still, I found that the literature about examples and applications is really insufficient. With that premise in mind this book has focused on providing step by step creation of a dynamic component capable of displaying different materials, open doors in both directions, and able to show different options so that designers can create their own libraries.

5
Matching models to photos

In many instances you will have a picture that you want to reproduce in a 3D model. Match Photo allows you to create a model to match a photo or to match an existing model to a photo's context. When you work with SketchUp you are using the actual, real-world scale. However, digital pictures are not at a 1:1 scale. Therefore, to create a 3D model that matches a photo (or to match an existing SketchUp model to a scale in a photo), you must calibrate SketchUp's camera to match the position and focal length of the digital camera used to take the picture.

Creating a model from photos consists of 4 high-level steps:
- Take digital pictures.
- Start matching: Matching involves loading a digital picture and calibrating SketchUp's camera to the position and focal length of the camera used to take the actual photo.
- Start sketching. Once you have duplicated the position and focal length of the camera used to take the picture, you can draw over the image in SketchUp.
- Repeat steps with any photos representing other views of the model.

Content

5.1 How to take digital pictures

Your success with Match Photo depends on the quality of photographs taken of your model:

- Take photos at a roughly 45 degree angle to each corner of the model. In an interior room this requirement is not always possible. However, try to set your shot from a point of view that allows you to see depth and length as close to 45 degrees.
- Do not crop photos; the point at which you aimed the camera should be in the center of the image. Also, when you crop images vertical lines will not align well and the results will be unsatisfactory.
- Do not warp photos.
- Remove barrel distortion or issues where straight lines are bent away from the center of the image. Barrel distortion typically occurs on wide-angle lens cameras. Use a third-party product to eliminate barrel distortion from images before using them within Match Photo. All cameras have a little bit of this distortion and it is typically worse around the edges of the image.
- Avoid stitched images.
- Avoid foreground elements.
- Avoid vanishing points at infinity although this is not a common issue in interior design.

Avoid front pictures

Take photos at a roughly 45 degrees

5.2 How to match the camera calibration to create a 3D model from photo

This process is best suited for making models of images containing features with parallel lines. Open the Components window and type "Kitchen5.2 by agra". Click on the word link to open the 3D Warehouse and choose the save option. Save it in your computer, open the file.

Details

1. The file that you just downloaded contains a picture of a kitchen that has been inserted by Camera > Match New Photo. When you select Camera / Match New Photo a background image file dialogue box is displayed. Navigate to the photo that you want to work with. Click the Open button. The photo will appear in the drawing area on its own scene in SketchUp. You are also placed in a matching mode where you will calibrate SketchUp's camera to duplicate the position and focal length of the camera used to take the actual photo. The words 'Match Photo' appear in the upper-left of the drawing area. Finally, the Match Photo dialogue box appears. Since the file that you just downloaded already contains the image, click on **Camera** > **Edit Match Photo** > Ikea Kitchen to open Match Photo window.

2. Click and hold the cursor on the origin   . The cursor changes to a hand.

3. **Move** the cursor to the front corner of the island. Release the mouse button. The origin is established.

4. There are four vanishing point bars in matching mode: two red bars and two green bars. Each bar is represented as a dashed line with square bar grips at the end. **Click** on a red vanishing point bar grip   . The cursor changes to a hand.

5. **Move** the cursor to the starting point of a position on the photo representing a line parallel to the red axis, such as the lower back corner of the island. **Zoom in** if necessary. Release the mouse button.

6. Click on the other red vanishing point bar grip. The cursor changes to a hand. **Move** the cursor to the ending point of the position on the photo representing the line parallel to the red axis.

7. **Release** the mouse button. The first axis bar is aligned to the red axis.

8. **Repeat** steps 4 through 7 for the remaining three (one red and two green) vanishing point bars. Following is an image of the matching mode after all the vanishing point bars have been aligned to axes. Note that in the picture the blue axis has been corrected by tweaking the green and red axis.

9. Click on the blue axis. A two-way arrow appears. **Drag** the cursor up to adjust the scale larger or down to adjust the scale smaller. You can use a 2D person as a guide as the person that appears in all new SketchUp files or any geometry with real world dimensions. Place the component in the origin and if the object is smaller than the island, move the cursor up to adjust the person or the geometry to be proportional with the size of the island. Instead of using any geometry you can bring a cabinet from your libraries and place it in the origin. Then move up or down to match with the desired height.

Note: To insert any geometry you will need to leave the match photo edit mode by clicking in a blank area of the screen or click on the Done button of the Match Photo dialogue box.

10. **Right-click** > Done or click on the Done button in the Match Photo window. You are placed in a sketching mode.
11. If you used a cabinet or a 2D person to scale the photo, erase it.

Note: If you Orbit or use any Camera tool you will not be able to see the picture anymore. Only the existing geometry will show. If at any point you get out of Match Photo mode click on the scene tab. To bring back the Match Photo dialogue box right-click on the scene tab > Edit Matched Photo.

5.3 How to use the matching process to create a 3D model

Once you have set the camera calibration you are placed in a sketching mode. This mode, unlike normal SketchUp drawing mode, is a 2D drawing mode. The words "Match Photo" appear in the upper-left of the drawing area and the Pencil tool is active. There are three sets of controls that are accessible during sketching mode. These controls are: The SketchUp drawing and modification tools, a few of the Match Photo dialogue box controls, and the sketching context-menu items.

Details

1. Sketch on photo using the SketchUp drawing tools: Use the **Pencil** tool to trace over the edges that make up the front-most side of the island in the photo. Trace faces following the red, green and blue directions and add edges being sure that you are always On Face when you are tracing. You probably will be off in some faces with the photo due to the picture distortion.

2. If you orbit around you will leave the Match Photo mode and you will able to see the 3D model with no picture in the background. To return to Match Photo mode click on the **scene tab** KitchenMatchPhoto.

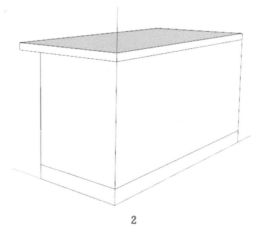

1   2

3. Continue drawing with the pencil tool to complete the island and then continue with the front face of the kitchen cabinets. Orbit around to leave the Match Photo mode and complete the missing faces. At this point you can enter depth dimensions for the cabinets and any other known dimensions.

4. Add detail as necessary.

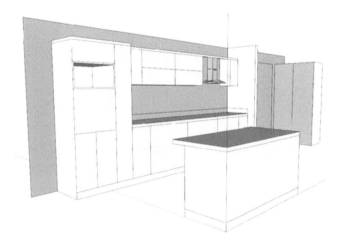

5. Select faces > right-click > **Project photo**. The message "Trip partially visible faces?" appears. Press the **Yes** button if you want textures applied to the portion of faces that are  shown in the image. Press the **No** button if you want textures applied to the entire face, even if the face is only partially shown.

6. Select each face > right-click > **Texture** > Position. Use the **Fixed Pins** method to shear and place the texture in the correct position. The best results are reached when you have many pictures from different angles to complete Match Photo on every single face.

Note: To re-enter matching mode select the photo you were matching from use Camera > Edit Matched Photo sub-menu or right-click on the Scene tab for the photo you were matching and select Edit Matched Photo.

5.4   Matching models to photos

Use the matching process to match an existing 3D model to a photo's context. For example, you might have a model of a kitchen island and want to place it within a photo to show the change. To match an existing 3D model to a photo's context you need to take a digital picture of the location where you will place your model. After opening your model the picture must be placed inside it.

Details

1. Download from the 3DWarehouse Kitchen 5.4 by Agra and open as a new file. Click on the island scene tab.

2. The next step should be **Camera > Match New Photo** to select the background image file. For the sake of this exercise you will click on the kitchen54 scene tab.

3. You are placed in a matching mode where you will calibrate SketchUp's camera to duplicate the position and focal length of the camera used to take the photo. The words 'Match Photo' appear in the upper-left of the drawing area. The Match Photo dialogue box appears. If not, right-click > **Edit Matched Photo**.

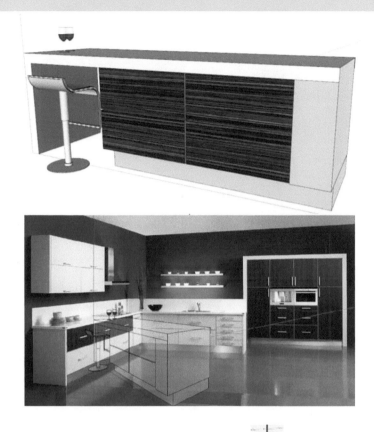

4. Click and hold the cursor on the origin 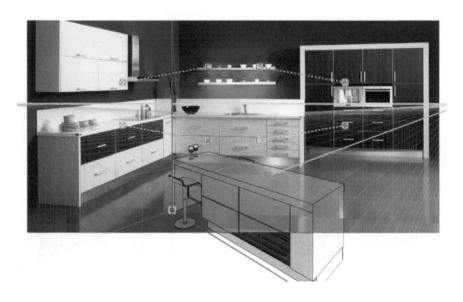. The cursor changes to a hand.

5. Move the cursor to the floor line matching the same depth of the cabinet on the left.

6. Release the mouse button. The origin is established.
7. Uncheck the **Model** checkbox in the Match Photo dialogue box. The model will be hidden. You can find Match Photo dialogue box in Camera menu > Edit Match Photo.

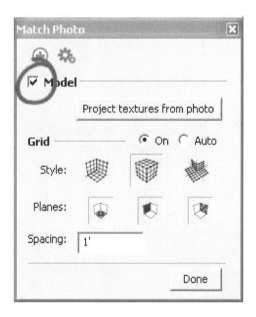

8. As explained before there are four vanishing point bars in matching mode, two red bars and two green bars. Each bar is represented as a dashed line with square bar grips at the end. Click on a red vanishing point bar grip ⬛. The cursor changes to a hand.
9. Move the cursor to the starting point of a position on the photo representing a line parallel to the red axis, such as the intersection of the wall with the ceiling. Zoom in, if necessary. Release the mouse button.
10. Click on the other red vanishing point bar grip. The cursor changes to a hand. Move the cursor to the ending edge of the cabinet in the front.
11. Release the mouse button. The first axis bar is aligned to the red axis.
12. Repeat steps 8 through 11 for the remaining three (one red and two green) vanishing point bars.
13. Turn on the model in the Match Photo window. Click on the blue axis bar. A two-way arrow appears. Move the cursor up or down the axis to scale the island. Adjust the blue axis to match the left cabinet height.

Following is an image of the matching mode after all of the vanishing point bars have been aligned to axis.

14. Right-click > Done. You are placed in a sketching mode. This mode, unlike normal SketchUp drawing mode, is a 2D drawing mode. Orbit Tool, Position Camera Tool, Walk Tool, and Look Around tool force you out of Sketch-Over-Image mode into normal SketchUp drawing mode. Click on the scene tab to return to Sketch Over mode.

15. If you want to complete the rest of the geometry proceed as explained in item 5.3. Keep in mind that the purpose of this exercise is just to match a model with a photo not to match materials between them.

6

Creating seamless and tiled materials

  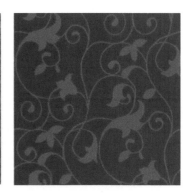

Kitchen design also includes the placement of organic materials or tiles in backsplashes and floors. Preparing textures for SketchUp is a simple task. In many cases it is necessary to be able to "tile" the texture over a larger region than the texture segment covers. In the ideal case the texture segment automatically tiles, that is, if it laid out in a grid it forms a seamless appearance. Therefore, you must consider the dimensions and how the texture will be repeated to cover a surface. There are two main groups of materials that you probably will face during the creation: seamless or tiled materials.

In both cases the material creation process starts from a digital image usually obtained from the real world. When it comes to a seamless texture the based image must have an even light and the four sides should match with the next repetition. The images for seamless textures are the most difficult to get. They usually must be retouched in an image editor to avoid the "patterned" repetition.

Tiled textures form such seamless surfaces easily because they are naturally bounded by rectangular discontinuities like grouts. Usually an image with four tiles and their grouts will be enough for a uniform repetition. The only factor to consider is to eliminate glare and contrasts of light because otherwise this effects will be repeated as many times as the image is repeated on a surface.

Content

6.1 How to create a tiled material

At the beginning of the process if you have taken a picture of the material to be incorporated into SketchUp is likely that you have to analyze what portion of the photo you are going to crop it since that piece will be repeated over and over covering a face. That is why you should avoid parts of a picture that are stained, have concentrated light areas or have perspective distortion. Another variable to consider when cropping a portion of a picture is to incorporate as part of the tiled material half the width of the exterior grouts to match it with the next repetition. When saving the image in your image editor for subsequent use in SketchUp do not exceed 300 pixels. This will avoid big file sizes.

In the present exercise the perspective distortion has been removed with Photoshop. There are some programs and tools that can help you in preparing the images for a good texturing like:

http://www.blitzbasic.com/Community/posts.php?topic=46368
http://www.seamlesstexturegenerator.com/
http://www.pixplant.com/index.php

Details

1. If you are taking a picture with a digital camera avoid big perspective distortions.

2. Open your image editor and correct perspective distortion to get a flat image. Correct brightness, contrast, and imperfections. Crop the portion of the image that you are going to use as a pattern.

3. Save the image in your computer and open SketchUp.

4. **Type** "Kitchen6.1 by Agra" in your Components window. Save it in your computer and open the file.

5. Open the In Model Materials window in the Edit tab > Edit texture image in external editor to open the image in your image editor. You can also right-click on the image > Texture > Edit texture image.

6. Observe that TiledImage.jpg has only small tiles on two edges while the SketchUp file shows a continuous pattern both horizontally and vertically. Identifying the pattern to be repeated to cover a surface is the key to the creation of such textures. Once the pattern is defined you will be able to apply it to any face and the texture will be repeated until the entire surface is covered.

7. Close your image editor and return to the SketchUp file. Save the material if you want it for future use as explained in Chapter 2.1

Tip: Sites containing free textures such as CGtextures.com or sketchuptexture.blogspot.com offer a vast array of suitable textures for interior design.

6.2 How to create a seamless material

For organic materials such as wood or granite where each part of the material is unique, a perfect result is almost impossible unless you have a picture of the whole area to cover. However, there are techniques to improve the appearance and avoid the tiled result using programs like Photoshop. Type "Kitchen6.2 by Agra" in your Components window. Save it in your computer and open the file. In these first steps you are going to save the image that is used in this exercise to observe the results. Repeat step 5 of the previous exercise to work with the image in your own photo editor.

Details

1. This image is a portion of a photo of granite chosen randomly. Observe in your image editor where the arrow points to a cloud belonging to the same material. This natural imperfection is not too noticeable in small areas. However, when the texture is used to cover larger areas this small difference becomes much more noticeable as you can see in the first rectangle on the left of the SketchUp file.

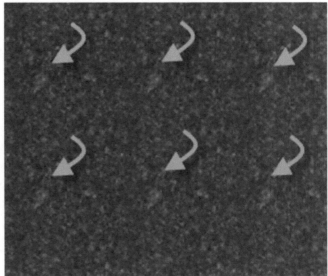

2. One way to correct these imperfections is by simply applying the Clone Stamp tool in Paint.net or Photoshop (to mention two different softwares) and re-save the image. The result will be similar to the second image rectangle in the SketchUp file. You can still see the tiled appearance, but it is much less noticeable.

1   2

3. A technique which is also applied to achieve better results is done in Photoshop following these steps.

1. Open the source image in Photoshop. Click on Image > Image Size, and noted what the image size is. You will need that information in the next step.
2. Then click on Filter > Other > Offset. Enter half the height value, and half the width value of the image in the offset values. Select Wrap Around. This action shifts the edges of the image to the center, and the center of the image to the edges.
3. To disguise the seams in the center use History Brush Tool (Hotkey Y). This brush is used instead of painting in a specific color as it paints with the original part of the image. You can also use Clone Stamp.
4. Paint over the seams. Avoid painting straight lines to fade off those seams in a natural way.
5. Now that you have a first draft of your seamless texture, it is a good idea to use Photoshop or SketchUp to tile it for you so you can make sure it tiles nicely. To do this in Photoshop select Edit > Define Pattern from the main menu. Write a name.
6. Create a new image that is several times larger than your original. With the new image selected select the Fill tool from the Edit menu > Fill.

7. Select Pattern under the "Use" drop-down menu and your newly created pattern as the Custom Pattern. Once OK is clicked Photoshop will tile your texture automatically.
8. If there are any parts of the image that stand out in the tiled image, you can go back and work on them a little more before finishing.
9. Save the image.

Note: You can combine this technique with another that involves mirroring each second segment so that adjacent edges match, as illustrated below. The larger segment can be repeated in the normal way indefinitely as all the edges will join without discontinuities.

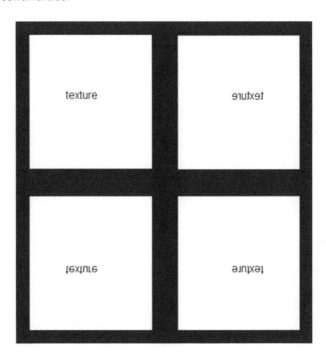

6.3 How to create a patterned texture

Repeating pattern files are also popular for wallpapers or fabrics. Patterns come in all shapes and designs, from vintage wallpaper to simple stripes. Whatever pattern you are creating the same simple steps apply. Zoom in and pick a focal point on the design. Drag out a marquee until you reach the same point elsewhere on the design. Crop the image to size then make duplicates to check whether the file matches and creates a seamless pattern.

Note: In case you have a scanned image such as a fabric, take the measurement of the real world sample to introduce that value in the Edit tab of the Material window. If by chance you had to crop or add some pixels to the original image to match with the next tiled image, you will need to add this measurement to that value too.

6.4 Mapping Plugins

Plugins that provide a new level by mapping textures in Sketchup are of invaluable help when applying materials.

The first one, called Thrupaint by Fredo, resides within a suite of tools that Fredo calls FredoTools. You have four ways to apply your UV texture: Quadmesh UV, Natural UV, Projected UV, and Transfer UV. These methods give you good control over how you want to texture your mesh. You can also choose to paint only front faces, back faces or both. The plugin offers another set of parameters for edges to which you want to apply a material. One of the strongest features is that you can apply a material to a component's face without the need to enter the edit mode. This feature is extremely useful when applying a door face image to different faces within a group, such as the exercise developed in chapter 2. This tool is extremely fast and very intuitive.

The second plugin is SketchUV by Dale Martens. SketchUV makes mapping easy for any user level. The toolbar is limited to just two buttons, a mapping tool and a path select tool, but within the mapping tool there are other options, such as view based and UV based. The plugin offers 6 mapping methods, but for kitchen design you will use Planar, Cylindrical and Spherical most of the time.

Having both plugins added to the native Paint tool of Sketchup will expand the ability to map almost any texture used for kitchen design.

7

Preparing your construction documents

If you plan to draw a model and take it to the contractor/builder for construction or estimate, you will need to know how to create styles, prepare your scenes, insert texts and apply dimensions. Selecting the appropriate style is a variable to consider. In your approach with the client you probably will show your design in full color and using perspective views. Whereas if you must prepare drawings for the manufacturer, the presentation will be completely different, probably without color and sectional views.

As you have noticed most of the elements inside your kitchen model are components. Assigning dimensions and text to these components can optimize your time substantially. Using texts and dimensions in SketchUp is quite easy. For those with the Pro version it can be even easier with the help of LayOut.

This chapter will cover a variety of subjects and will highlight some tips to improve your efficiency.

Content

7.1 Creating a new style and preparing your scenes

The Section Plane tool is particularly useful in presenting interior spaces. In kitchen design you can, for example, create a horizontal section plane to show base cabinets and another horizontal plane for the wall cabinets. You can also create for each elevation a new section plane. Usually sectional views are represented in black and white and are used for professional work. The Monochrome face style of SketchUp can be a good start to create a new style that can be saved for future use. This style uses thickened edges to indicate cut-through faces, but as with all the styles in SketchUp it does not fill in the areas between them. The following exercise will show you how to create a new style and solve this issue. If your model is composed of a large number of faces avoid the use of "sketchy" styles since that will require more computer resources.

Details

1. Open the kitchen1.10 file saved in the first chapter.
2. **Select** the "Left" scene tab.
3. Select View > **Face Styles** > **Monochrome** to check that all faces are oriented so that the back-side is facing out. To make it easier to see the "reversed" faces open the Style window in the Edit tab. Click on the Face Settings button and change the back color to black. (You can move the slider down to reach the black area).

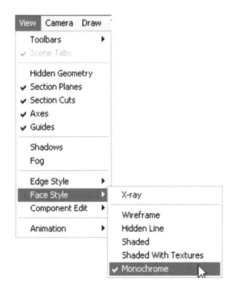

4. All back faces will show in black. Double-click on the black faces until you reach their edit mode > right-click > **Reverse Faces**. Set the cut-through faces back-sided so they show in black.

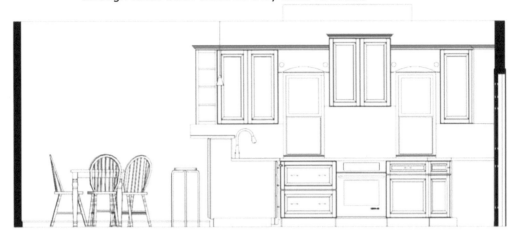

Tip: There are two useful plugins. One named Reverse Back Face in the Ruby Library Depot that reverses the back faces in the view of an exploded model. Therefore, it does not reverse faces within components and groups. So if you are planning to use it run the plugin before converting any geometry into a component or a group. The plugin installs in the File menu.

The second, even easier, resides within the FredoTools. The tool tells you whether you are in the presence of a front or back face and can be used with exploded geometry or within components with no need to enter to the edit mode.

5. The thickened-edge effect that makes section cuts stand out looks too heavy when combined with the poché d in-between areas. Make them thinner by selecting the **Modeling** Settings tab of the **Styles** dialogue box. Set **Section cut width** to "1".
6. In this same section of the Styles dialogue box, uncheck Section Planes.
7. Click on the Edge Settings button and set Profiles thickness to "1" and Depth Cue to "2". This allows curved or multi-faceted surfaces to appear outlined and emphasizes the lines of geometry in the foreground over the lines of geometry in the background.
8. If you want to show in dashed lines the inside of your cabinets check the Back Edges o   n.
9. Click on the   button to create a new style and call it "Section Cut". Open the **In Model** styles to check that the new style was added. Right-click on the thumbnail > **Save as** > save it in your hard drive for future use.

10. To be able to print or work in LayOut you need to create Scenes. Without setting up scenes in your SketchUp model, there's no way to assign a specific Section Cut to a viewport in LayOut. Open the **Scenes** window and create a new one called "Elevation1". At the prompt save it as a new style.
11. **Select** the "Rear" scene tab.
12. Open the **In Model Styles** window and select the Section Cut style. Reverse faces if needed.
13. Create a new scene. Name it "Elevation2".
14. Save as Kitchen7.1

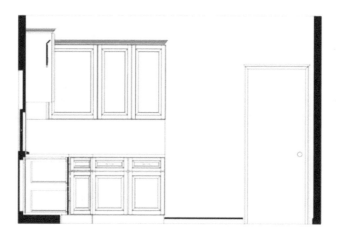

A scene is not a snapshot. A scene will keep the camera position and the settings but not the geometry. A scene is a set of view settings that are automatically updated to reflect your changes. You can create scenes and delete them all through your design process. As you noticed creating scenes is a simple process. The idea is that you add a scene whenever you have a view you want to return to later. To activate a scene you added earlier double-click the name of the scene in the Scenes dialogue box or single-click the tab for that scene at the top of the modeling window.

Note: There is a plugin called Section-Cut Face, developed by TIG, that automatically generates filled-in outlines for the section cuts. It is available at Sketchucation.com. You need to register in order to have permission for the download. Once downloaded, install the plugin inside the SketchUp's Plugins folder and restart the program. After creating the section plane, select it, right-click (Ctrl-click on Mac), and select Create Section Faces in the contextual menu.

7.2   Configuring text settings

The text settings can be done through the Model Info window located in the Window menu and by selecting the Text panel. In that window you will see two sections: Screen Text and leader Text. The Screen text contains characters, is not associated with an entity, and is fixed to the screen regardless of how you manipulate or orbit the model. If you use this type of text and then use the Pan or Orbit tool the text will remain fixed and will not follow the model. You can, however, move this text. To insert a Screen text, click in a blank area of the screen and then type your text. Click away from your note when you are finished.

For annotations use the Leader Text. This text contains characters and a leader line that points to an entity. There are two styles of leaders: View Based and Pushpin. A View Based leader will always retain its 2D screen orientation. A Pushpin leader is aligned in 3D space, and rotates with your model as you change your view. Whereas view-based text disappears when its leader line is hidden, pushpin text remains visible even when its text or leader is partially hidden. View-based text is appropriate for presenting still shots like an elevation. Pushpin text is good when you want all texts available at all times. You can specify which type of leader is used from the Text panel of the Model Info dialogue box.

Details

1. Open Kitchen7.1 file.
2. **Window** menu > **Model Info** > **Text >** Leader text section. Click on **Fonts...** button and select Tahoma option. Notice the two check boxes on the top right corner of the window. Selecting the Height option will provide you extra control if you are intending to print in a scale. This option works pretty much as in a CAD program and is relative to drawing units. The size you type in is the real word dimension. So if you intend to print in a ½" = 1'-0" scale, a reasonable size will be 3" that will turn into a 1/8" printed size. A way to calculate this is to take the final output size and multiply it by the scale factor that for ½" scale is 24, 48 for ¼" and 96 for 1/8". In this example if you multiply 1/8" by 96 you will get as a result 3" for the starting size. The Points option sets the text size related to the screen; so it always shows the same size on screen whether you are zooming in or out.

3. Select the Height option and enter 2″ in this case. Click on the OK button.
4. Choose Dot for the Leader lines end point.
5. Choose View Based for Leader. Close the Model Info window.

7.3 Leader Text

As mentioned before Leader text contains characters and a leader line that points to an entity. When you click on the Text icon, the cursor changes to an arrow with a text prompt. By clicking on any entity you are indicating the ending point of the leader line. If you point to a component, the leader will show the name of that component which is also shown in the Outliner. Pointing to a line or a surface the leader text will give you information about the edge or face.

If you want to take advantage of this action, name or rename your components in the Outliner the way you want them to appear in the construction plans. It can be a cabinet reference, a generic description or the cabinet width.

Since the information presented in each view or scene is different, working with different layers devoted to text is recommended. By creating a different layer for text appearing in elevations, sections, and floor plans will allow you to hide them according to the view you are working on or printing.

Details

1. Make the Elevation2 scene active by clicking on the scene tab.
2. **Create a new layer** in the Layers window and name it "Tx_elev". Make it current.
3. With the Select tool double-click on the wall cabinets group to enter the edit mode. Select the **Text** tool .
4. Move the cursor to position the text. The leader line will grow and shrink as you move the cursor around the screen. **Double-click** to create a text line with no leader.
5. A text entry box appears with the name of the component.

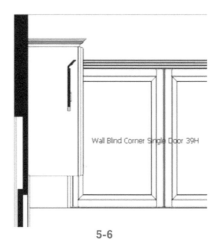

5-6

6. Type \n followed by a space 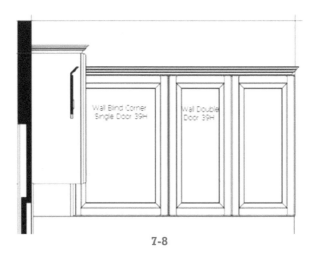 where you want to start a new line of text (Microsoft Windows). Press the **ESC** key at any point during the operation to start over or to cancel.
7. Click outside of the text box, or press the **Enter** (Microsoft Windows) or **Return** (Mac OS X) key twice, to complete text entry.
8. Repeat with the remaining wall cabinets.

7-8

Tip: Annotations can be included during the creation of a component. Assigning a separate layer is recommended. When you import or reuse in a new project a component that has been set in this way the texts can be made visible by checking the corresponding layer and therefore there is no need to type it in the new model.

To edit the text, double-click with the Text tool or Select tool active. You can also context-click on a text entity and select the Edit Text menu item from the text entity's context menu. Be aware to right-click close to the insertion point; otherwise the context menu will not show.

While Text command is active you can move any text object. You could also use Move tool for this.

To change any text properties open the **Model Info** window, select the text that you want to change, choose your new settings and then click the button **Update selected text**. You can select all text objects at once by clicking on the **Select all leader text** button.

7.4 3D Text

While the 3D text is typically used in instances where you want to create a text as geometry, it can also be used as an alternative to Screen text. The advantage of this option is that a geometric object will have a spatial location within the model that does not vary. This option is of particular interest when required to place a tag to a particular view. You should keep in mind, though, that since this is a geometric object it will appear in every scene. To avoid this situation put the text on the same layer assigned to the other texts and therefore seen only in the desired scene.

Details

1. Continue with Elevation2 scene.
2. Select the **3D Text** tool.
3. Type "Rear Elevation". Change the Height to 5". You can avoid introducing a height value since this is a geometric object that can be scaled in a later step.
4. **Uncheck** the Extruded option.
5. Place the text over a wall to fix the orientation.
6. Move the text below your elevation view.

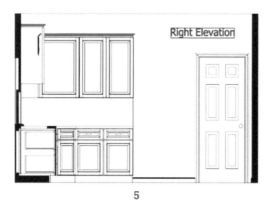

5

6

7.5 Configuring Dimensions settings

Dimensioning is an easy and intuitive task, but some factors must be taken into account especially if you are planning to export or print your model. Another chapter will cover the use of dimensions in LayOut for those who have the Pro version.

To control the way in which the dimensions appear in your drawing you have to select **Model Info** from the Window menu and then choose the option Dimensions. Just as with texts, you can change fonts, colors, endpoints, and the location of the value in relation to the string.

By default the dimensions are aligned to the screen. To make changes to dimensions drawn previously you can select all at one time with the button Select all dimensions, make changes and then click on the Update selected dimensions button. For additional options select the Expert dimension settings. Through this dialogue box you can control the display of dimensions when they become very small or foreshortened. With this last variable you could hide those dimensions that are not perpendicular to the active view. To control the units choose the Units tab of the Model Info window.

Details

1. Open the Window menu > **Model Info** > **Dimensions**. Enter to the Text section > Fonts > Select Height for the Size option > write 2" > OK.
2. Change the Leader lines to Slash.
3. In the Dimension section> Align to dimension line > Above.
4. Click on the **Expert dimension setting** button > select "Hide when foreshortened" and "Hide when to small" options and keep the slider close to 25% from the left. Close.

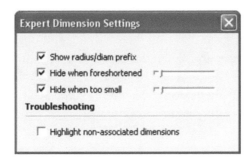

7.6   Inserting dimensions

You can find the Dimension tool on the Menu Bar, under Tools. Once selected, your mouse will turn into a white arrow, meaning that SketchUp is ready to take dimensions. To add dimensions simply select the two points of reference for the dimension and pull away. You can also select an edge and then pull to position the dimension. If your model is made of components, there are two ways of using this tool: you can edit the component and take advantage of all the features of this tool, or you can use it outside the component. Using the second method is recommended because editing a component and applying dimensions inside means having these measures reported in all the instances of the component. This could consume unnecessary computer resources.

When you are entering dimensions you must be careful to select appropriate reference points. If working in an elevation view or floor plan with a non-orthogonal geometry it is likely that reference points are not located in the same plane. Because of this issue you will learn to force a dimension band in a particular direction or it is recommended dimensioning in a 3D view and inferring with the given axes.

By default all dimensions are dynamically linked to the model, meaning that any change in the geometry result in a change to the associated dimension. To override the value of a dimension double-click the value and type the new value or text. This new information would not change even if the distance is changed. You can reestablish the dynamic dimensions by double-clicking again on the number, delete it, and followed by Enter.

Details

1. Continue in the Elevation2 scene.
2. Select View menu > Face Style > **X-Ray**
3. **Zoom in** the right side of the wall cabinet and click on the outside line of the cabinet.
4. **Pan** to the left side and pick the endpoint against the left wall.
5. **Hold down** the left mouse button to ensure a dimension in the ortho mode.
6. **Drag** your mouse up to locate the dimension band. Release.
7. **Turn off** X-Ray mode.

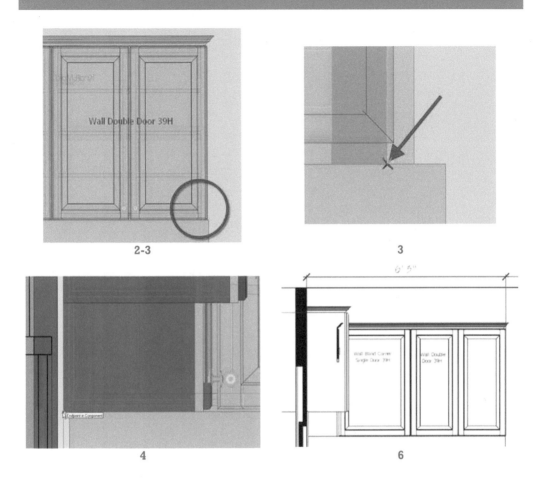

Note: You can always force a dimension in a particular direction if the two points of reference are not on the same plane or the same coordinate. By moving the mouse toward one direction you can get a horizontal dimension band.

8. Click on the "Walls" scene tab and orbit around to get an **iso** view from the door.

9. Select the **Dimension** tool and click in the top corner of the walls' intersection.

10. Click on the top left corner of the door frame while you hold down the left mouse button.

11. **Hold down** and **drag** your mouse up in the blue direction to obtain a horizontal dimension.
12. Click to position. If you are not able to see the dimension, check the configuration of the **Expert dimension settings.**

13. **Orbit** around and click on the bottom right corner of the wall cabinet.
14. **Zoom out** and click on the top corner of the right wall intersection while you keep holding down the mouse button.
15. **Move** the mouse in the blue direction and release it. Close the cabinet width dimension.
16. Return to the Elevation2 scene.

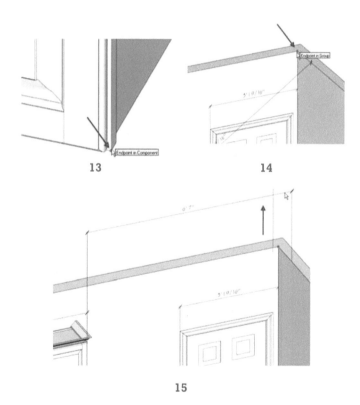

13

14

15

Note: A good trick to place dimensions in specific places is to create a section cut, align the view and pull out dimensions from the section cut. Another tip you can use sets a proper view of your dimensions. Shift the value one line up or one line down if it interferes with other dimensions. To do that, double click on the dimension to edit it. Then write <>\n or \n<> if you want the value displayed one line up or one line down. Click Enter to obtain the shift.

You can also use the edit mode to add a text instead of the dimension value. If you want to combine text and a dimension value, double-click and write "yourtext <>". The <> signs will restore the dynamic behavior of the dimension.

17. Using the concepts presented, finish entering the dimensions on the left side, inferring with the section cut endpoints.

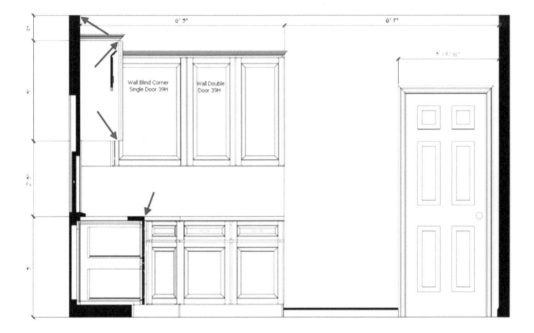

7.7 Changing settings from the Entity Info window

As it was mentioned before it is recommended that you use layers when you insert dimensions because you can turn them on or off depending on the scenes you are working on. Through the Entity Info dialogue box you have access to a certain number of options to modify the layout of your dimension. It is possible to change the font, the type of alignment, how the endpoints are displayed, and layers.

Details

1. **Select** all the dimensions in the Elevation2 scene > right-click > **Entity Info** > change the layer to Tx_elev.
2. Select the Floor Plan scene tab. Change the style to "Section Cut". Right-click on the Floor plan tab > Update.

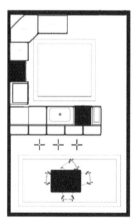

3. **Create a new layer** named TX_plan and make it current.
4. **Double-click** on the cabinets group to reach the instance of each cabinet component. Select the corner cabinet.
5. Open the **Outliner** and rename it "BA36L". The reference will be added at the beginning of the name. Repeat to rename the Base Single Door and the Base Double Door Double Drawer cabinets as shown in the picture.

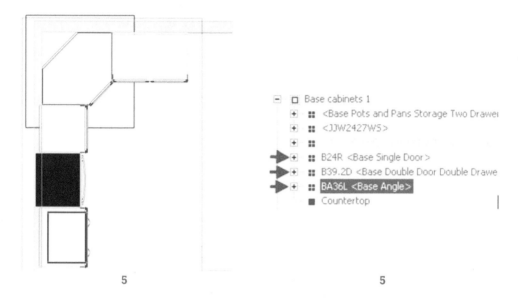

5   5

6. With the group in edit mode select the text tool and insert the reference name for each cabinet as explained in item 7.3.

7. **Close** the group. Open the **Layers** window make Layer 0 current turn on TX_plan and turn off TX_elev.

8. Open the **Scene** window, check all the properties options and then select Floor plan scene > Update button.

9. **Click** on Elevation2 scene tab > Open Layers window. Turn off TX_plan and turn on TX_elev.

10. **Select** the text that you have inserted before that reads "Right Elevation" > right-click: Entity Info > change the layer to TX_elev.

11. **Update** the Elevation2 scene.

12. **Save** the file as Kitchen7.6

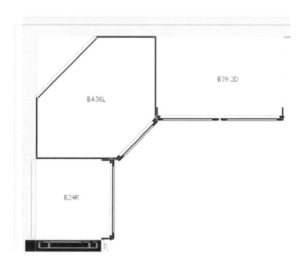

7.8 How to use LayOut to insert dimensions and texts

For those who have the Pro version, LayOut provides all the tools to explain, present, and insert dimensions in your 3D model quickly and accurately. Using the Dimension tool it is only a matter of picking the reference points and inserting the dimension where you want it to appear. You can set units, colors and fonts. When you are inserting dimensions they automatically snap to the SketchUp model entities. You can dimension your SketchUp model or a LayOut paper space.

As explained above, the first step to be successful in this task is to create scenes for each view of your model that you want to show in your document. You can use as many views of the same model as you want. When your file is modified in SketchUp, LayOut updates the file using the References pane in the Document Setup dialogue box.

After creating the scenes in SketchUp open LayOut and create a page to insert a viewport. The panels located on the right give you access to different configurations. Pages panel lets you move between existing pages. Using the SketchUp Model dialogue box you can specify which scene is linked to each viewport and assign the scale at which you want to print. Note that drawing scales apply only to non-perspective, straight-on views of your model. If you have inserted your dimensions directly into SketchUp, use LayOut for printing.

However, in this exercise you will practice how to insert dimensions directly in LayOut.

Details

1. Open **LayOut** and from the **Getting Started** dialogue box choose a Letter size template from the New tab. **Open**. (In Mac choose it from the Default Templates)
2. **File** > Insert > Browse for the kitchen7.6 file. Open.
3. **Open the SketchUp Model dialogue box** located at the right of your screen. Change Scenes on the View tab to "Elevation1".
4. Change the **Scale** to ½" = 1'-0". Check that the Ortho button is on.
5. Adjust the viewport dimensions by dragging the blue handlings.

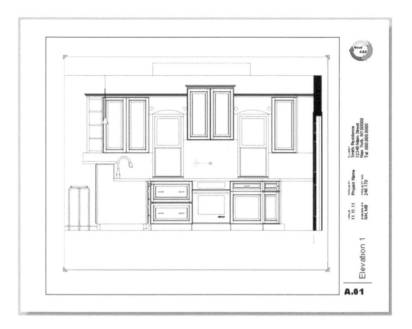

6. Select the **Dimensions** tool . Open the **Dimension Style** dialogue box. In this pane you can control units, precision and how the dimension styles will read. Change the length to Architectural and the precision to 1/8". Since you already scaled the viewport using the SketchUp Model window, turn on the Auto Scale button. If however you are drawing your own elements you have the option to set your own scale.
7. Open the **Shape** dialogue box and choose an option for the start and end arrow.
8. Open the **Text** dialogue box and choose a font and a color.
9. Click on two points of your model, in this case the higher cabinet between the two windows. Place the dimension string.
10. **Double-click** on the next corner of the next cabinet across the window to continue the dimension string.
11. **Double-click** again on the endpoint of the same cabinet to insert another dimension.

*Note: In order to snap dimensions to a SketchUp model you need to have active **Object Snap**. To access to this option, right-click outside your viewport window > Object Snap. If Object Snap is off it will not allow you to reference many points in your model.*

Dimensions created in LayOut and referenced to a SketchUp Model are tied to that model. Keep this in mind especially if you move or rotate your model.

*To adjust dimensions strings double-click and move it to a different position, change the point at which it is referencing or use **Alt/Opt** key to alter the angle. By double-clicking again you can change the text position independently from the dimension line.*

To insert a text instead of a value double-click and enter a new text. To reset it to a value again, double-click and erase the text.

To change the line type or stroke sizes use the Shape Style window. With the Style icon you can sample and change an existing setting and apply it to other elements.

Following the instructions that have been provided, insert all of the other dimensions.

12. Select the **Text** tool  and type "Left Elevation" in the paper space. Select the text and change size and font.

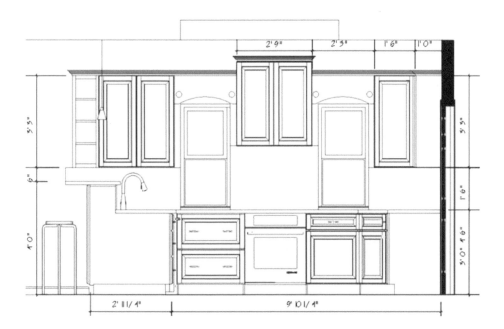

13. Finally, open the Pages window and click on the **Duplicate selected page** button ⊞. **Highlight** the new page and then select the viewport. Open the **SketchUp Model** window and change Scene to Elevation2. Note that although the scene changes, you still have the dimensions inserted in the first layout. That is because you have copied all the information of the first page. **Erase** the dimensions with the erase tool.

14. Also note that the sizes of the letters on the Elevation1 sheet are larger than in Elevation2 sheet. To resize the fonts you must return to the SketchUp model and make adjustments. After making these changes in the model they can be updated in LayOut. Open your model in SketchUp and click on the Elevation2 scene. Select **Model Info** > Dimensions from the Window menu.

15. Click on the **Fonts...** button. Change the Height to 3.5" > OK.

16. Click on the **Select all dimensions** button, and then click on the **Update selected dimensions**. Close the Model Info window.

17. Save your model and return to LayOut.

18. Open **File** > Document setup. In the dialogue box your model should appear in red. Select the Update button. Your file will update the changes in the Rear Elevation sheet.

19. **Open** now the Left Elevation sheet. Make a crossing window from left top corner to right bottom corner to select all the dimensions at once.
20. Open the **Text** Style dialogue box and change the size to 8.
21. **Save** the file. Return to SketchUp.

8

How to print and export your documents

SketchUp has some simple tricks to print images with sharp and clear lines. The simplicity of SketchUp is vastly different from what the alternatives offer. Typically, end-users will export an image and print in a photo editing program.

There are many printing options offered in SketchUp. The first aspect to consider is the output quality. By default, the quality of the Print dialogue box is set to Draft. Besides the output quality you will need to decide whether your printing is based on vectors or raster image.

Another element to take into account is if you are printing to scale or fitting to a page. SketchUp allows you to print your designs using any printing device. You can also print to scale and span a print across multiple sheets, allowing you to output a large drawing from a standard printer.

Content

8.1   Basic steps to print – Fit to page option

Printing directly from SketchUp, especially with the Fit to Page option, does not deviate much from the same procedure used to print in any other program. If you do not have the Fit to Page option selected you can manually enter a page size using Page size. These steps are usually followed when you want to print a raster image. In order to get sharp lines select "High Definition" in the drop down menu of the Print Quality. To print directly from SketchUp and get defined lines check the option "Use High Accuracy HLR" in the Print dialogue box. Using this feature will send the information to the printer to print as vectors instead of pixels. If you use this option please note that it is possible that the start of the printing takes several minutes depending on the complexity of your model. Do not use imported images "as images" because they will not be recognized; use only objects with textures. The option HLR also will not recognize shadows.

Details

Microsoft Windows

1. **Open** the file Kitchen7.6.
2. **Select** Alternative 1 tab.
3. **Turn off** layers Tx_elev and Tx_plan.
4. Use **Zoom Extents** to center the drawing in your window. By using this command you can center your drawing within your paper. If at some point you find that your drawing is coming out on several pages instead of being centered in the selected paper size, go back to your screen and use Zoom Extents. Note that if you have other entities inside your model using Zoom Extents will include them all in the active screen. In that case hide those entities or use Zoom Window, and in the Print dialogue box turn off the option Use model extents.
5. Open **File** > **Print Setup**. Choose your printer, paper size and orientation > OK.
6. Click on **File** > **Print Preview**.
7. In the **Tabbed Scene Print Range** section choose the scenes that you are going to print. If you have only one scene in this part of the dialogue box, it will not be enabled.
8. In the **Print Size** section choose **Fit to page**. The Fit to page option is used to size the model to fit on a single sheet of paper and will tell

SketchUp to make your printed page look like your Modeling Window. This option must be disabled to specify a different size or scale.

9. Check the **Model Extents** option to instruct SketchUp to zoom in to make your model fit the printed page. In case the program is not zooming in try to uncheck Model Extents, create a preview and then make a second attempt by checking the option again. If still does not work as expected turn this option off.

Note: As long as you do not have the Fit to page option selected you can manually enter a page size using Page size. If you type in a width or a height, the other dimension will be calculated. Use this option to make a larger picture by tiling together many smaller pages.

10. Click on the **OK** button. You will see an image of what your print will look like.

11. If you are satisfied with the result, click on the Print button. You can also close the preview window and then print your model using **File** > **Print**.

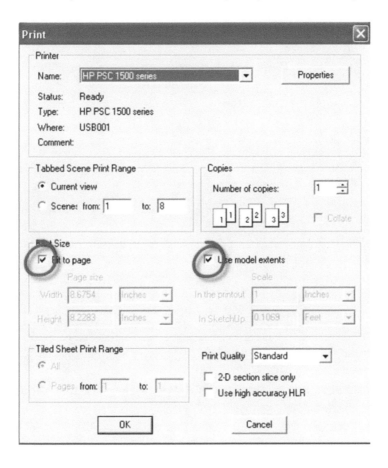

The Print Preview and Print dialogue boxes contain the same series of options. The only difference is that the Print Preview dialogue box outputs your model to the screen instead of to a printer. Items configured in one of these dialogue boxes automatically appear in the other dialogue box.

Details

Mac OS X

1. **Open** the file Kitchen7.6.
2. **Select** Alternative 1 tab.
3. Use **Zoom Extents** 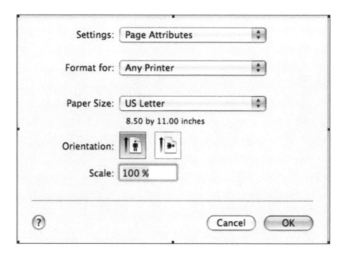 to center the drawing in your window. By using this command you can center your drawing within your paper. If at some point you find that your drawing is coming out on several pages instead of being centered in the selected paper size, go back to your screen and use Zoom Extents. Note that if you have other entities inside your model using Zoom Extents will include them all in the active screen. In this case hide those entities or use Zoom Window, and in the Print dialogue box turn off the option Use model extents.
4. Use **File** > **Page Setup** to select printer, paper size and orientation for your printer.
5. Click on the **OK** button.

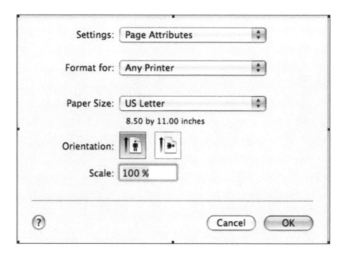

Settings:	Page Attributes
Format for:	Any Printer
Paper Size:	US Letter
	8.50 by 11.00 inches
Orientation:	
Scale:	100 %

Cancel   OK

6. Choose **File** > **Document Setup**. Make sure that the Fit View to Page check box is selected.
7. Click the **OK** button. Using this option will tell SketchUp to make your printed page look like your Modeling Window.

Note: As long as you do not have the Fit View to Page option selected you can manually enter a page size using Print size. If you type in a width or a height, the other dimension will be calculated. Use this option to make a larger picture by tiling together lots of smaller pages. The Pages Required section is readout of the number of pages you need to print. With the Fit View to Page box selected this should read:

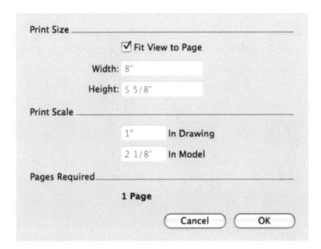

8. Use **File** > **Print**. Select 1 copy. If the Pages readout indicate that you need more than one page, you can choose to print some or all of them. In the Print dialogue box click the Preview button. If you are satisfied with the result, click on the Print button.

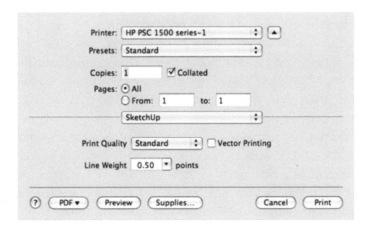

8.2 Printing to scale

Before printing to scale you have to set things up properly.

Since perspectives views cannot be printed to scale, you will need to switch to Parallel Projection on Camera > Parallel Projection. You can choose any standard view, such as Top view. When the size of the printout exceeds the printable area of a single page, SketchUp spans the printing across multiple tiled pages. You have the option to print all the pages, a specific single page or a specified range of pages. Usually printing large models to scale rarely presents a problem. Printing 1:1 models to scale may require resizing the SketchUp window. If this is your case, limiting the empty space around the model is the key to reducing the number of tiled pages required to print.

Besides adjusting the camera to a standard view (Top, Bottom, Front, Back, Left or Right) and Parallel Projection use Zoom Extents. This command centers the model in the drawing area and zooms to the closest view of the entire model.

Another requirement is to align your model to the drawing axes as well.

Understanding the Print Properties dialogue box has been for many end-users a challenge. Many forums contain printing advice. However, the lack of a clear explanation about how to solve some outcomes has caused a lot of frustration. Properties such as orientation and paper size are easily understood since they are common elements among all computer programs. Understanding the Print Size section where the scale and page size must be set will define the key to your success. The two most important settings are Fit to Page and Use Model Extents options. Fit to Page option forces the print output to fit a single page with no regard to scale. This option disables the Scale and Page Size fields and the Tiled Sheet Print Range section. If you want to print to scale you must deselect the Fit to Page option. Model Extents reduces the overall physical size of the print by discarding the empty space around the model. Using Model Extents does not affect the Scale of the print, only the overall size of the print resulting onto a single page or the number of required tiled pages. Margin settings can influence your final result. For example if your drawing is 8.5" wide and you are printing in a 8.5" letter size paper, SketchUp will tile your drawing onto two pages since the margin must be considered as part of the width of your drawing.

Presenting documents for a kitchen design involves raster images as vector based drawings as well. For your vector based documents check the option Use

High Accuracy HLR. Using this feature will send the information to the printer to print as vectors instead of pixels. If you use this option please note that it is possible that the start of the printing takes several minutes depending on the complexity of your model. Images, textures and shadows will not recognize with this option. Vector based drawings can also be printed with the High Definition property of the Print Quality drop-down box and sometimes takes less time to be processed than the HLR option.

Details

Microsoft Windows

1. Continue working with the same file.
2. **Select** the "Elevation1" scene tab. This scene is in parallel projection.
3. Use **Zoom Extents** to center your drawing in your window. Using this command will enable you to center your drawing within your paper. If at some point you find that your drawing is coming out in several pages instead of being centered on the selected paper size, go back to your screen and use Zoom Extents and try a different paper Orientation.
4. Choose **File** > **Print Setup**. Select your printer, Legal for paper size and Portrait for orientation. Note that you are selecting Legal size paper instead of Letter size; otherwise the drawing does not fit at the selected scale in a Letter size paper. Click on the OK button.
5. Select **File** > **Print Preview**. By default Fit to page and Use Model Extents are checked. As it was explained before you must deselect the Fit to Page option to be able to print to scale. Using Print Preview to see what you are about to print, will save you time, paper, ink and frustration. At this point, note the gray cells. The Tiled Sheet Print Range section should show the number 1 indicating that only one page is needed. The Scale section indicates a value slightly less than 2. This value shows the biggest scale to which you can print for your drawing to fit on one sheet. For example in a later step if you change this value to "1", the Tiled Sheet Print Range will show the number of required tiled pages. If you change the scale to ¼" = 1'-0" this value will be "1" again. Keep this information in mind as it will help you to adjust the setting to print to scale. When the size of the printing exceeds the printable area of a single page, SketchUp spans the printing across multiple tiled pages. You have the option to print all the pages, a specific single page or a specified range of pages. By default, the print range is set to All and the Pages from-to fields display the total number of pages the print requires.

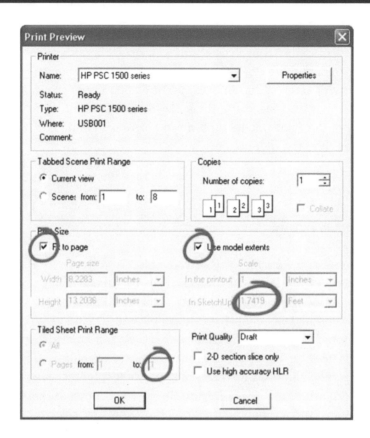

6. Uncheck the **Fit to page** option and **Use model extents**. The values of **Tiled Sheet Print Range** will change showing that you need more than one sheet. Check **Use model extents** option again. The paper size will be recalculated and the **Tiled Sheet Print Range** will show one page again. The **Use model extents** option is used to print only the model as viewed using the Zoom Extents tool. This option might discard any surrounding empty background. If in your first attempt the number of pages needed is not reset, close the dialogue box, apply Zoom Extents command and reopen Print Preview dialogue box. Use Model Extents generally reduces the number of tiled pages when printing large models. Printing small models may bring up some issues resulting in a print that takes many more pages than necessary. To solve these inconveniences you can manually resize the SketchUp window to minimize the empty space around the model.

7. Enter a "2" in the **In SketchUp** field. The Scale fields are used to scale your model for printing. The first measurement, labeled **In the printout**, is the measurement of the exported geometry. The second measurement, labeled **In SketchUp**, is the actual measurement of the object in real scale.

8. Enter the scale at which you would like to print. If you want to print at 1/2″ = 1′ you have to enter "1" Inches **In the printout** box and "2" Feet into **In SketchUp** box. Do not pay attention to the numbers that appear on the Page size option when you are printing to scale. The Page Size fields display the overall size of the printing, not the size of the paper. When you enter values in the Scale fields, the program calculates the dimensions of the print output and displays the resultant width and height in the Page Size fields. Use this information as a guide to whether the printing will fit within the printable area of the paper.

The Page Size values do not update automatically when entering values in the Scale fields. Uncheck and recheck the Use Model Extents option to refresh the Page Size fields.

Here are some common scales configurations:

Architectural
½″ = 1′. Enter 1 Inches; 2 Feet
¼″ = 1′. Enter 1 Inches; 4 Feet
3/16″ = 1′. Enter 3 Inches; 16 Feet
1/8″ = 1′. Enter 1 Inch; 8 Feet

Engineering
1″ = 20′. Enter 1 Inches; 20 Feet
1″ = 50′. Enter 1 Inches; 50 Feet
1″ = 100′. Enter 1 Inches; 100 Feet

Metric
1:20.= Enter 1 Meters; 20 Meters
1:50 = Enter 1 Meters; 50 Meters
1:100 = Enter 1 Meters; 100 Meters

Note: If you want to select a different size paper, change the settings in File > Print Setup. If you do not want a tiled result the only option is to select a smaller scale. When the current scale is larger than the paper size of your printer or plotter, the entire model can be printed by printing on several pieces of paper. These pieces of paper can then be taped together to create the final scaled model. For example, tiling lets you print proofs of a large model, such as a B size (11″ x 17″), on a printer that uses a smaller paper size, such as an A size (8.5″ x 11″). Page tiles are numbered top to bottom beginning at the top left of the drawing page. Printing large tiled output can be taxing on your computer's resources.

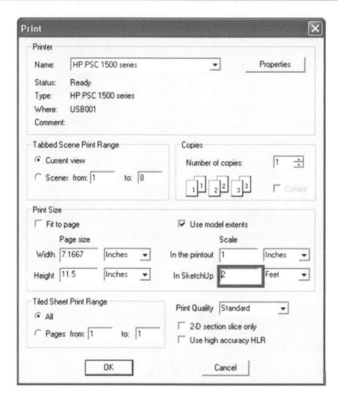

9. Select Use High Accuracy HLR (vector printing) to compare with the performance of printing with the option that you did in the past exercise. Print quality menu is disabled when the HLR option is selected. Note the Use High Accuracy HLR printing option does not support printing images, only colors, and sometimes do not print some lines. Deselect Use High Accuracy HLR when you want texture images to appear in the printout.
10. Click the **OK** button and if you are satisfied click the **Print** button. You can also close the preview window and then print your model using File > Print.

Mac OS X

1. Continue working with the same file.
2. **Select** the "Elevation1" scene tab. This scene is in parallel projection.
3. Use **Zoom Extents** to center your drawing in your window. Using this command will enable you to center your drawing within your paper. If at some point you find that your drawing is coming out in several pages instead of being centered on the selected paper size, go back to your screen and use Zoom Extents and try a different paper Orientation.

4. Choose **File** > **Page Setup**. Select your printer, Legal for paper size and Portrait for orientation. Click on the OK button.
5. Select **File** > **Document Setup**

Take note of how many pages your drawing needs by checking this information in the Pages Required area on the dialogue box. If you want to select a different size of paper change the settings in File > Page Setup.

6. Uncheck the **Fit View to Page** option.

The Scale fields are used to scale your model for printing. The first measurement, labeled In Drawing, is the measurement of the exported geometry. The second measurement, labeled In Model, is the actual measurement of the object in real scale. Enter the scale at which you would like to print. If you want to print at 1/2" = 1' you have to enter 1 Inches **In the printout** box and 2 Feet into **In SketchUp** box.

Look for the most common scale configurations in the Microsoft Windows settings.

7. Click the **OK** button.
8. Open **File** > **Print**. Click on the **Preview** button and if you are satisfied click the **Print** button.

8.3   Exporting a PDF file

Another way to print or share your files is by exporting to other programs. You will be able to export your files in 2D and 3D. If you use the Free Version you can export 3D models to other programs in several 2D and 3D formats like JPEG image (.jpg), Portable Network Graphics (.png), Tagged Image File (.tif), Windows Bitmap (.bmp). You can also export your files to COLLADA (.dae) format for use in a variety of different 3D programs. You can also export animations and walkthroughs as MOV with the Mac version of SketchUp, or export AVI files from the Windows version of SketchUp.

In addition to everything you can do with SketchUp®, using SketchUp® Pro you can export in additional 2D formats like Portable Document Format (.pdf), Encapsulated PostScript Format (.eps), Epix (.epx), Autocad® (.dwg, .dxf). The 3D formats are 3DS (.3ds), Autocad® DWG (.dwg), Autocad® DXF (.dxf), FBX (.fbx), OBJ (.obj), XSI (.xsi), VRML (.vrml). The PDF and EPS export is used to export vector SketchUp files for use in other vector-based editing programs, such as Adobe Illustrator. Some graphic features of SketchUp, including textures, shadows, smooth shading, backgrounds and transparency, cannot be exported to PDF and EPS.

Details

Microsoft Windows

1. **Select** the "Elevation 1" scene tab. This scene is in parallel projection.
2. Select File > **Export** > 2D Graphic > Select **PDF** for Export type.
3. Enter a file name for the exported file in the "File name" field.
4. Click the **Options** button.

   - Full Scale (1:1) option is used to set your output to a 1:1 (real world) scale. Width/Height: are used to enter a custom page size for your file. In Hidden-Line Output/In SketchUp fields work the same as the printing on scale.
   - The Profile Lines section of the PDF/EPS Hidden Options dialogue box contains options for exporting profile lines. Show profiles exports any lines that are displayed in profile as thicker lines in the 2D vector file. All lines are output normally, without profile thickness, when this option is disabled, regardless of the screen display. Match screen display (Auto Width): automatically sets the width of profile lines by matching the output to the proportions you see in the SketchUp drawing area.

- The Width fields are used to specify an exact width for the profile lines. This option is available only when "Show Profiles" is checked and "Match screen display (auto width)" is unchecked.
- The Section Lines section contains options for exporting section lines. The Specify section line width option is used to adjust settings for Section Slice lines that are output. The Match screen display (auto width) automatically sets the width of section lines by matching the output to the proportions you see in the SketchUp drawing area. This option is available only when Specify section line width is checked and "Match screen display (auto width)" is unchecked.
- The Extension Lines section of the PDF/EPS Hidden Options dialogue box contains options for exporting extension lines. The Extend edges option is used to toggle the export of line extensions. The Match screen display (auto width) automatically sets the width of extension lines by matching the output to the proportions you see in the SketchUp drawing area. The Width fields are used to specify an exact width for the extension lines. This option is available only when "Extend edges" is checked and "Match screen display (auto width)" is unchecked.
- The Always prompt for hidden line options is used to automatically display the Hidden Line Options dialogue box when you export a 2D PDF or EPS file. The Map Windows fonts to PDF base fonts is used to select PDF fonts that correspond to the Windows fonts used in the model.
- Defaults: This button is used to return the items in the Hidden Line Options dialogue box to the default settings.

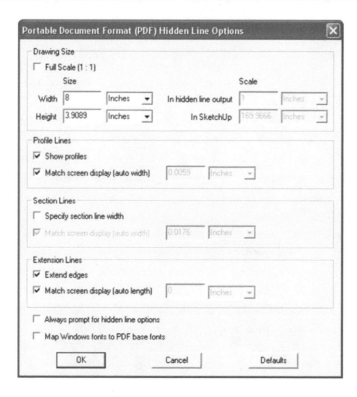

5. Accept the default options > OK.
6. Click the **Export** button.

Details

Mac OS X

1. Select File > **Export** menu item. The export dialogue box is displayed.
2. Enter a file name for the exported file in the "Save As" field.
3. Select **PDF** from the Format drop-down list.
4. (Optional) Click the Options button. The PDF Export Options dialogue box is displayed. Refer to the PDF Export Options dialogue box (Microsoft Windows) for further information.
5. Click the **Save** button. The images are saved and then displayed in your current PDF viewer (by default).

8.4 Exporting Image files

If your intention is to print or use an image of your model in any photo editor you will need to export an image selecting the adequate resolution for your printing purpose.

Details

1. Select File > **Export** > select any image file extensions from the Export type drop-down menu.
2. Enter a file name for the exported file in the "File name" field.
3. To change the resolution options click on the **Options** button to select a different image size. Keep in mind that a good resolution for printing is 300 dpi, meaning that for every inch that you want to print you have to multiply it by 300. For example, a 8" wide image will have a size of 2400 pixels.
4. Click the **Export** button.

8.5 Exporting 2D DWG or DXF files

This is a **Pro** only feature.

Details

1. Select File > **Export** > 2D Graphic. The Export 2D Graphic dialogue box is displayed (Microsoft Windows).
2. Enter a file name for the exported file in the "File" name (Microsoft Windows) or "Save As" (Mac OS X) field.

Note: If you want to export the 3D geometry you will need to select File > Export > 3D Model.

3. Select the DWG or DXF export type from the "Export type" (Microsoft Windows) or "Format" (Mac OS X) drop-down list.
4. (optional) Click on the Options button. The DWG/DXF Hidden Line Options dialogue box is displayed.
5. (optional) Adjust the options in the DWG/DXF Hidden Line Options (Microsoft Windows) or Export Options (Mac OS X) dialogue box.
6. (optional) Click the OK button.
7. Click the Export button.

8.6 Printing from LayOut

If you have the Pro version you can use LayOut to insert your drawing. The main concept between SketchUp and LayOut is that the first one works in a 3D environment and the second is like working with paper. You only pay attention to scale in SketchUp when you intend to print. LayOut defines scales and paper size more clearly. You can use LayOut to present SketchUp models, both on paper and on-screen. You can also export your documents in PDF format. The result can also be more beneficial since in the SketchUp model tab of LayOut you can choose instead of Vector the option Hybrid. In that way you can have the advantages of printing as well as raster and vector. The lines will be crispy while you will be able to print shadows and images. However, bear in mind that texts inside a component in many instances will not show when printing.

Details

1. **Open** the LayOut file that you used in item 7.7.
2. Open the **Pages** panel. **Duplicate** one of the pages shown inside the list. **Click** on the drawing to access to the viewport frame.
3. Open the **SketchUp Model** panel and change Scenes to Floor plan. Note that your drawing is not fitting inside the boundaries of your paper even by resizing the viewport when the scale is specified to ½"=1'-0". Change the scale to 1/4" = 1'-0" (1:48).

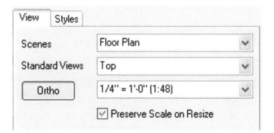

4. **Adjust** the viewport to the new dimensions of your drawing and center it in the page.

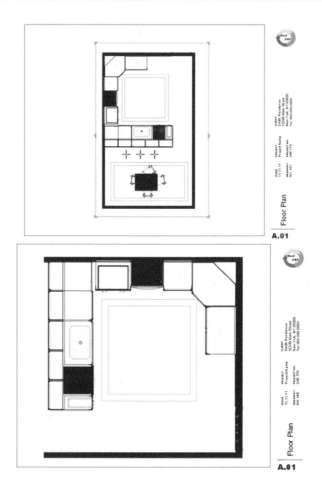

Note: In case you want to stay with the ½"=1'-0" scale you will need to either change the way your drawing is displayed or change the paper size in File > Document Setup > Paper. In this dialogue box you can change paper size and margins to fit your drawings at the desired scale. You will also need to change your template. If you select the first option you can for example keep a sheet with the ¼"=1'-0" scale and have another sheet showing a detail. You can also rotate the model to fit with the paper orientation and resize the viewport to the portion of the drawing that is important to show. Above are two images that explain this concept.

5. Choose File > **Print Preview** (Windows) **/File > Print > Preview** (Mac). In this panel you can check the outcome of all the pages in your LayOut document.
6. Select File > **Print**. In this dialogue box choose the page to print.
7. Click **OK** to send your document to the printer.

8.7 Creating a PDF file in LayOut

A second option in LayOut would be to export your file in PDF with an output in High Quality. This alternative allows you to print anywhere or share your file with somebody else.

Details

1. Select File > **Export** > **PDF**. If you are on a Mac, choose File > Export and then make sure PDF is selected in the Export dialogue box. This opens the Export PDF dialogue box.
2. **Name** your PDF file.
3. Click the **Save** button (Windows) to open the PDF Export Options dialogue box; click the Options (Mac OS X).
4. Set the PDF options.
   - Page: In the Page section choose which pages you want to export. Accept defaults.
   - Quality: When your documents are Letter or Legal size use High for Quality. For anything bigger, select Medium or Low options. Set the option to Medium.
   - Layers: PDFs can have layers, just like LayOut documents do. With this option you can export a layered PDF so that people who view it can turn the layers on and off. Uncheck this option.
   - Finish: Select this check box to view your PDF after it is exported.
5. Click on the **Export** button. Click OK on Mac to close the PDF Export Options dialogue box and then the Save button.

Note: when you want to print something from LayOut that involves Section Cuts you need to create a style specifically for the scenes that show your Section Cuts as explained in chapter 7. Also, do not display section planes in your style unless you want them to show up in LayOut.

Use separate Scenes for each section plane so they can be shown in LayOut independently. Without setting up scenes in your SketchUp model, there is no way to assign a specific Section Cut to a viewport in LayOut. Deselecting the Section Planes checkbox in the Modeling Settings section of the Edit tab in the Style dialogue box is the key to making sure your Section Planes are invisible. When the appropriate style is applied to your scenes, you are ready to assign them to different viewports in LayOut.

8.8   Complete your drawing in LayOut

LayOut has drawing tools that can help to complete 2D drawings such as the arches that show how to open doors. You can also overlap objects to correct unwanted effects obtained from a section cut. LayOut defaults to a black stroke (line) and white fill, for all entities, by default. To change the fill and stroke used for all new entities select Window > Shape Style.

Details

1. Select the Arc tool ⟍ and draw the door opening.

2. Select the Rectangles tool ⬚ and draw a rectangle overlapping the black door opening.
3. Save.

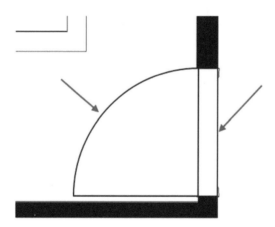

8.9   Other LayOut tools to get good results

The **Rendered** button in the SketchUp Model dialogue box allows to re-render a model when you have made a change to it that invalidates the current rendered image, such as when changing the style. Re-rendering can take a long time if your model is large. Use the Rendered button to re-render a single, large, model. Check the 'Auto' checkbox to re-render an entire document containing many large models. This operation could take several minutes to several hours so uncheck the checkbox if you do not want further automatic rendering updates. The Rendered button's label will change to 'Rendered' when the currently selected model has been re-rendered.

The **Rendering Mode** drop-down list contains three options for rendering your models on screen and in output format.

- Vector: Use the Vector setting to display and output all lines, faces, and text in a vector format. Features such as texture, fog, and shadows will not display in this mode. Vector is appropriate for large, orthographic output. The vector setting provides crisp and scalable line work that can efficiently scale up to very large paper sizes. It cannot render with all of SketchUp's raster rendering capabilities, and it can be performance intensive to generate renderings of complex SketchUp models.
- Raster: Use the Raster setting to display and output all lines, faces, and text in a pixel-based format. The Raster setting can render a model exactly as it appears in SketchUp, though it can be cumbersome and performance intensive at high resolutions and large paper sizes.
- Hybrid: Hybrid renderings take the longest to process, but they provide the best final product.
  The hybrid setting provides a hybrid rendering method that combines the sharp, scalable line work of vector rendering with the richer capabilities of the raster renderer.

The **Camera Settings**
If you need to change any Camera settings of a scene, you can access to the Context menu by right-clicking on an entity or viewport > Edit 3D View > Right-click > Camera tools > Select an option.

9

Tips to add some lighting effects

To achieve lighting effects, shadows, and brightness many designers would resort to any rendering engines or plugins that are available in the market. However, on many occasions designers need to discuss and view preliminary ideas with their clients. Repeatedly returning to rendering software can be time consuming and is not cost effective. So when it comes to indoor spaces there are some tricks to incorporate lighting to let in the sunlight, the only light source provided by SketchUp.

As it was mentioned in Chapter 1.12 one way lies in giving the ceiling a not-cast-shadows property through the Entity Info window. While this is a fantastic idea many times it falls short when combining natural and artificial lighting. You can manipulate the projection angle using the sliders of the month and hour, but may not be able to achieve the desired atmosphere. In this chapter you will practice how to manipulate the sunlight, work with transparent faces and add some glow effects with free software.

Content

9.1   Non-cast shadows ceiling

Non-cast shadows ceilings in SketchUp is a trick to illuminate interior spaces. The Shadows window allows manipulation of the shadows by the day and time of year. Those shadows are projected with a certain inclination, depending on the time zone in which the model is located. This configuration is of vital importance when you are doing a study of shadows to see the impact of the entry of sunlight into an interior space. However, sometimes creating "unreal shadows" helps to add contrast to the model.

Details

1. **Open** Kitchen1.10 and select the "Left" scene tab.
2. Switch to Camera > **Perspective**.

3. Activate the **Walk** tool and walk forward until you get an interior perspective.

4. **Create** a new scene. Name it "Perspective".

Note that if you Turn off Display Section Cuts you will probably see the wall instead of the interior. When you turn on Display Section Cuts and Shadows, the sunlight will also enter to the indoor space coming from this part of the model depending the orientation and time. If you want to have an enclosed space allowing the sunlight to enter only from the ceiling surface you can change the parameters in the Shadows window and the Field of View to allow a wider view angle and approach the model in a closer perspective. For the sake of this exercise you will work with the Display Section Cut option in On mode.

5. **Select** the ceiling group > right-click > Entity Info > check off "Cast Shadows".

6. Open the **Shadows** window and turn shadows on _____.

7. Open Window > Model Info > **Geo-location** > Set Manual Geo-location. Change the Latitude and Longitude to 0.0 to allow vertical shadows.

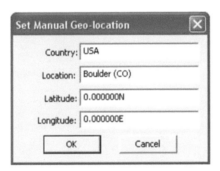

8. Change the Shadows settings as shown in the picture by changing the UTC +/-0. Slide Time and Date sliders to allow shadows as vertical as possible.

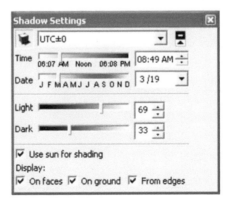

The resultant shadows will look similar to the picture below.

Tips to add some lighting effects

9.2   Ceilings with transparent materials

When it comes to letting the sun enter the interior space you can use a combination of other methods than non-cast shadows. SketchUp has the capacity to have different materials on each side of a surface with the ability to hide the edges of the faces. Painting the outward-facing surface with a material whose opacity is less than 50% and on the other side using an opaque material allows you to control the entry of light. Making a comparison with what was explained in the previous exercise, applying a transparent material to the outward face of the ceiling would have almost the same results as non-cast shadows properties. However, when applying a translucent material in specific areas natural and artificial light cones emanating from light fixtures can be simulated to great effects.

In the next exercise you will add geometry with a transparent material applied on the outside ceiling surface to allow passage of light.

Details

1. Continue with the same file used in item 9.1
2. Turn the **shadows off** to manipulate the model faster.
3. Select the ceiling > right-click > Check **Cast Shadows and Receive Shadows**.
4. Change to an **Iso** view and **turn off Display Section Cuts**.
5. **Double-click** on the ceiling group to enter the edit mode and draw two guide lines, one at 3'-6" from the left edge side, and the other at 9'-0" from the bottom edge side.

6. **Draw** three circles with 12" radius, 30" apart each other.
7. Still in the edit mode apply a **translucent material** to the three circles. Erase guide lines.
8. Close group and return to **Perspective scene** tab.

9. **Double-click** the ceiling again to enter to the edit mode. Apply to the inward circle faces the same texture as the rest of the ceiling.

10. Turn the **shadows** on  and apply similar settings. You will note circular light sources on the peninsula countertop. The intensity of the light depends on the material where it is displayed. You may wish to change the countertop material to a lighter texture to enhance the lighting difference.

11. Type in the **Components** window "Hanging Light by Agra" and insert it in the center of the three circles of the ceiling.

12. Select the three lamps > right-click > Entity Info > check off Cast Shadows. This step is to avoid cast shadows of the lighting fixtures on the light projections. Open the **Outliner** and drag the three lamps inside the ceiling group.

13. Double-click the ceiling again and select **Erase tool + Shift key to hide** the circle edges. This command will keep the circles and the light sources but the edges will not be noticeable.

14. **Draw** a rectangle matching the center space of the kitchen. If you have drawn a coffered ceiling from the beginning you can draw something similar as shown in the below image. **Apply** a yellow translucent material to mimic a light fixture.

15. Close the ceiling group and **turn on shadows**. Note the light source on the floor.

16. **Update** the Perspective scene and save as Kitchen9.2.

9.3 How to use transparent materials to simulate light source projections

As previously noted, in the interior design field artificial lighting is vital and in SketchUp, the sun is the only source of illumination. Recreating shining light sources is impossible when using only SketchUp. In the past two exercises you practiced a few tricks to get some sunlight inside an interior space. To add an additional accent you can recreate artificial lighting by "faking" light source projections. In this exercise you will download a conical light projection, place it in the model and observe the way it is built.

Details

1. **Search** in the Components window "Light Projection by Agra" and download it inside your model.
2. **Place it** below the Hanging Light as shown and **copy** it for each of the fixtures.

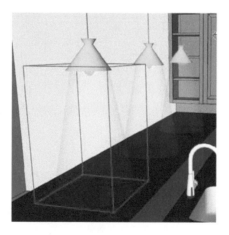

3. Open View menu > **Component Edit** > **Hide Rest of Model** to allow viewing the component isolated from the rest of the geometry when you enter to the edit mode.
4. **Double-click** on the Light Projection component to enter to the edit mode, and turn on View > **Hidden Geometry**.
5. Sample the cone texture with **Paint Bucket + Alt/Command** and look in the **Edit** tab of **Materials window** to see that the material has translucent properties below 50% in every single face. Bear this in mind because higher values cast shadows. Also observe that the top and bottom circles of the cone were hidden by using Erase tool + Shift key. Watch that there is a second component that has less translucency and

a more intense color to simulate the light bulb. The component has a small vertical line to provide an endpoint that when it is inserted. Using Window> Soften Edges only the faces were exposed.

6. **Turn off** View > Hidden Geometry.
7. **Save** as Kitchen 9.3.

Note: The shapes of the light cones are governed by the type of lamps and shades you are using; this is why a good advice would be to keep different light projections options for each type of light fixture that you usually use.

9.4 Adding glow properties in an image editor

To give a touch of sparkle from the lights you can use any picture editing program like Photoshop. In this exercise, the procedure done with Paint.net, a free software, to apply "illuminated" lights. Basically, you will create a new layer, select the Gradient toolbar, select the Diamond and Radial gradient tools and drag from center to the point where you would like the fadeout to end.

Details

1. **Open** file Kitchen 9.3 and export an image by File > Export > 2D Graphic > Choose a JPEG extension and provide a name > Export.
2. Open your image editor, in this case Paint.net (to use another software than Photoshop). Open the image.
3. Layer > **Add New Layer**.
4. Layer Property > Blending mode > **Glow** or **Overlay** > Opacity > 255.
5. Select **Gradient** tool > **Diamond**. For the primary color choose a RGB 255,240,173 with a 70% of transparency value. For the secondary color choose a RGB 255,252,244 with a total transparency
6. Apply glow below the hanging lamps and the cabinets. You can combine with some touches of the Radial brush too.

Tip: While applying the Gradient tool select the areas where you want to apply the effect to avoid touching other unwanted surfaces

ABOUT THE AUTHOR

Adriana Granados is an independent writer and author of SketchUp for Interior Design and Space Planning book series. She has concentrated on the application of information and communication technologies in the field of interior design and architecture. She is a leading software instructor at the college and private levels especially for interior design. For several years she was the Latin American support for various software programs related to architecture and interior design and trained hundreds of people in the use of different architecture software. She is actually the CEO of a company that provides outsourcing of drafting and rendering services worldwide, works as a designer, has a blog where she shares tips and ideas and is a permanent contributor in Sketchucation online magazine. With degrees in interior design and architecture and a strong entrepreneurial background she is able to cross over between her artistic and technical capacities.

CPSIA information can be obtained
at www.ICGtesting.com
Printed in the USA
LVHW070410300319
612422LV00028B/568/P